# LIFE AMONG THE MOONIES

# LIFE AMONG THE MOONIES:

## Three Years in the Unification Church

*by*

*Deanna Durham*

**Logos International
Plainfield, New Jersey**

Scriptures are quoted from the following versions: *The New English Bible* (NEB), copyright © 1961, 1970 by Oxford University Press and Cambridge University Press; *The Jerusalem Bible* (Jerusalem), copyright © 1966 by Darton, Longman & Todd Ltd. and Doubleday & Company, Inc.; and the *New American Standard Bible* (NAS), copyright © 1960, 1962, 1963, 1968, 1971 by the Lockman Foundation.

**LIFE AMONG THE MOONIES**
Copyright © 1981 by Logos International
All rights reserved
Printed in the United States of America
Library of Congress Catalog Number: 81-80395
International Standard Book Number: 0-88270-496-6
Logos International, Plainfield, New Jersey 07060

# *Dedications*

To all those who prayed that I would find the truth, especially my mother, who prayed faithfully for three years, even during the times when she felt overcome with hopelessness. Also to my cousin Lois Torrence and her church, who prayed with great concern.

## *Contents*

Preface  **i**
1 How Did It Begin?  **1**
2 The Advent of Darkness  **14**
3 Caught in the Maelstrom  **29**
4 Disguised as an Angel of Light  **42**
5 The Trap Snapped Shut  **59**
6 But What About the Children?  **69**
7 The Death of Compassion  **78**
8 The New Beginning?  **89**
9 Follow the False Hope  **99**
10 Respite  **113**
11 Darkness Reigns  **126**
12 The Battle Explodes  **153**
13 Advent of the King  **173**
Epilogue  **199**

# *Preface*

I wrote this book with much prayer and the hope that my sharing of these experiences and those of my children will touch others with the powerful love God has for each of us.

This is an account of those things which happened to me when I was a member of the Unification Church. I have changed most names to protect the privacy of the individuals involved. The situations described were unique to my experience, but they touch a chord of commonality in the experiences of many who have been involved with the group.

The writing of this book has been a process through which the Lord has healed my life in a miraculous way, and, as a result, I have been in constant awe of the direct contrasts between darkness and light in our world today. The manner in which I was deceived by the misuse of Scripture and love has become very clear to me.

I pray that the reading of this book may keep others from falling into the same trap of deceit. Jesus said that we must judge a tree by its fruit, and that a good tree cannot bear bad fruit. I offer my experience as a test of the fruit of the Unification Church.

There are many members of the Body of Christ who have helped to make this book possible by their concern and ministry of love. I want to thank all of them from the depths of my heart. But there are several people who have helped in a very concrete way.

My thanks go to Bob R. for his indispensable help in checking the mechanics of this book. Great thanks also go to Marge T., Kathy R. and Betty D. for their help in typing the final copy of the manuscript. My deepest thanks go also to my husband and my children for their encouragement and patience during the many hours I spent writing.

Again, I pray that this book will be an encouragement to all who read it because of its testimony to the unfathomable love of the one true God for each and every person, no matter how far he may have strayed from the truth. Jesus Christ offered His life as a fulfillment of God's will, and to free all mankind from bondage. All anyone has to do is to ask, and he will receive the full salvation which He has bought for us.

# LIFE AMONG THE MOONIES

# 1

# *How Did It Begin?*

It was indeed a new day. My whole being was newly alive with the knowledge of the truth of love. It was as if all of creation was in celebration with me. The gentle warmth of the sun, the brilliant song of the flowers, the soft caress of the breeze—all of these were calling me to the celebration of God's goodness and lovingkindness.

It was June 27, 1976, and I was about to be married. This was not such an unusual event in itself, but if you consider that only five months before, I had not cared whether I lived or died, this day truly was a miracle of God.

In the preceding months, I had slowly emerged from a dark cloud of hopelessness, anger, hurt, and resentment. I had been to the point of trusting no man, and even more desperately, of not even trusting God, to whom I thought I had given my life. My life had been so full of desperation that I had come to the conclusion that I could not even tell the difference between God and Satan in my life anymore.

And now, on my wedding day, my life was filled to overflowing with the joy, the kindness, the tenderheartedness, the understanding, the very fullness of God's love in my life. What had happened to me during those five months? The answers had been revealed to me slowly and with great care, like a flower unfolding, through God's Word, the Bible. The whole essence of His love was summed up to me that day in the Scripture which was read at the marriage ceremony: "Love is patient; love is kind and envies no one. Love is never boastful, nor conceited, nor rude; never selfish, not quick to take offence. Love keeps no score of wrongs; does not gloat over other men's sins, but delights in the truth. There is nothing love cannot face; there is no limit to its faith, its hope, and its endurance" (1 Cor. 13:4-7, NEB).

I had spent the preceding three years of my life in one of the most deceitful imitations of love that can be imagined. I had been a member of the Holy Spirit Association for the Unification of World Christianity, better known as the Unification Church, or commonly known as the Moonies. I had been intensely devout in my belief in the doctrines and messiahship of the cult's Korean founder, Sun Myung Moon. The story of my journey into the strange, even mysterious, world of the "family" of Sun Myung Moon involves a series of struggles, agonies, furtive joys, deep relationships, fears, and a desperate search for God—all of which, for me now, seems unbelievable. This whole experience in the Moonies led me to total disillusionment and torment.

About a year before I first encountered the Moonies, my marriage was in very deep trouble because of mutual immaturity and selfishness. I had been going to a psychologist for counseling and had been told by him and by a physician that I was suicidal. I had not taken this very seriously, but I was taking a large number of tranquilizers every day to keep me going.

Then the bombshell dropped; I found out I was expecting our first child. However, because of our strained marital situation and my deep emotional problems, I realized I was in no way ready for this responsibility. I was deeply afraid for the marriage, for myself, and mostly for the baby. On one particular afternoon, when I felt completely overwhelmed by my fears, I began taking a good look at the rest of my life and realized I had almost completely turned away from God. This was a shocking realization since I had, from childhood, been very aware of Him and His workings in my life. It was at this point that the Lord reminded me of something I had done several years before.

Before I was married, at a time when I was desperately afraid that my fiancé was going to abandon me, I remembered saying aloud, "Dear God, I know this is wrong, but right now, I want him (my fiancé) even more than I want you. Please let me marry him." As I recalled this incident, I was filled with shock and despair and realized that nothing had been really right in my life since then.

The Lord opened my eyes at that moment, and I saw that His love was the only thing that was really of any importance in the whole world. I prayed, for the first time in quite awhile, a prayer of deep and earnest repentance. Then I gave my life to God. "O Lord, your love is the only thing that has any value in this world. Everything else must come from that. Please God, if you will only let me have your love, I will do anything for you!" From that moment I felt stronger, and I realized I was also experiencing a feeling I had not experienced for a very long time—hope.

Slowly my life began to change, and I began attending

church alone every Sunday. I had attended the Episcopal church for many years before I stopped going to church, so that is where I began to attend once more. I remember the hour in church as being the high point of each week. Each time I went, I felt the overwhelming presence and love of God. But after a while, I found myself in quite a dilemma, because my heart was aching to experience His presence all the time, not just in church on Sundays. My husband and I began attending a marriage experience class during the week, but this was not enough. I would strain to listen carefully to everything that was said at the services on Sundays, because I was certain I must be missing something. The sermons were geared to the social gospel. Although they were very helpful in guiding my actions, I seemed to be getting nowhere in my relationship with God.

Meanwhile, my son was born. He was a beautiful and healthy child. We named him Joshua because the name means, "God is my salvation." My marriage situation seemed to settle down for a while, yet I was feeling more and more restless in my search for a growing relationship with God.

It was at this time that I began a search that was based on curiosity as well as a desire to know the truth. My interest was caught by such things as astrology, the I Ching, ESP, and other occult subjects. I was becoming increasingly aware of powers beyond the everyday, explainable things, and wanted to know more about these forces and where they came from. I thought that possibly they could be the link that would bring me closer to God. Thus, I read everything I could get my hands on that had anything to do with understanding God or supernatural powers. Strangely, with all the reading I was doing, it never occurred to me to pick up the Bible. Although I heard the Scriptures every Sunday at church, no one ever talked much about the Bible. My personal attitude was that the Bible was interesting historically, but I really did not have any awareness that it could possibly pertain to my life in these days. I did believe it was from God, but I thought its only application was that it showed the truth about what had happened long ago. I sometimes read the synoptic gospels, little bits at a time, and they gave me a very deep love for Jesus. There was no doubt in my mind that He truly was the Son of God, but I could not exactly discern how any of the rest of the Bible would apply in helping me know God in a deeper way.

By the time Joshua was about a year old, my search for a growing relationship with God had become quite frantic. I decided I was just not able to get the answers I was seeking at my own church, so I began systematically to visit all the churches in town. Before I could put my new plan into action, however, an event took place which changed my entire outlook.

When Joshua was about five months old, I accepted a job as an assistant instructor in remedial reading at a night school program in adult education and, as it turned out, I was put in charge of the reading program for the night school. I enjoyed this job very much, because I met many interesting people and gained a tremendous amount of self-confidence.

During the spring of 1972, when Joshua had just turned one year old, I was asked by my superiors to attend a reading workshop in Reno, Nevada. They were quite anxious that I go, and they were sending several other members of the staff from the day program as well. So, arrangements were made for me to go to the three-day workshop. The program was unusually interesting, and I made some new friends. One of these was a young man named Dennis, who was in charge of the reading program for the day school.

We found that the workshop was to end on Friday at noon, and because of some unforeseen problem, we could not get a flight home until Sunday. We all met at one of the motel rooms to decide what to do with our free time. Some of the people wanted to go to the casinos, and some wanted to go for a drive. But Dennis and I did not want to take part in either activity. We had gotten into quite a deep discussion and did not want to end it, so we stayed behind. It turned out that Dennis had been on a search somewhat like mine, and as we talked, it became evident that we both had had some very strange and wonderful experiences with the Lord before our marriages.

While either talking about or meditating about God, for example, we had both experienced spiritual states which seemed utterly foreign. These were states in which the presence of God would become so overwhelming that we would find ourselves almost totally overcome. In my case, these experiences had always resulted in teaching from the Lord. At first the teachings had been very elementary; for example, the first time, I experienced the wholeness of the creation and the love with which God had created all things. This was not an intellectual understanding—but an actual experiencing in my heart—of the truths He was teaching me. Usually when this happened, it would last an hour or two and then fade away. Later, I related it to experiences I had had with drugs. But the experiences with God were much clearer because they involved the presence and love of God which caused them, not any synthetic substance. Most had taken place while I was in the company of another young man to whom I was very close at the time. The last of these experiences was the most amazing; it occurred late one afternoon in the fall of 1968. This particular young man and I were having chili at a small restaurant near my school's campus. We began talking again about God and trying to figure out what His will was for our lives. I said, "I really feel the Lord wants to do something specific with my life." He agreed that he felt the same way. I then said, "I have had the feeling lately that the Lord is going to come again soon, maybe even in our lifetimes."

He replied, "Yeah, I feel like what He wants me to do has something to do with that."

"Wow, I've felt the very same way," I answered. Just as these words left my lips, I was filled with an energy which I cannot explain. It was as if I had received a powerful surge of some electrical force. I was stunned and the presence of God became almost tangible. I was looking straight into my friend's eyes, and a split second after this force swept through me, he jumped up and began backing toward the door. He later said that he felt God's power come over me, and that it seemed to travel from my eyes to his. He was terrified, and tried unsuccessfully to look away. He began to back away, but he could not get away from it. The whole experience ended just as abruptly as it had begun, but we both felt that it strongly confirmed what we had been feeling about the Second Coming of Christ. It was not long after this occurrence that I became engaged and married, and my experiences with God subsequently lay dormant for several years.

As I related these events to Dennis, I was relieved to

hear that he had had some similar experiences before his marriage. As we talked, we both realized that God's presence was practically tangible in the room, and I began to cry in gratitude to God for letting me experience this tremendous closeness to Him again. We both felt as if our eyes had been opened, that we could see the love of God in the creation and that we could understand His love in our hearts; yet, as we went out walking through the town, we could also feel God's pain at the sin of man. It was almost unbearable to experience these things at such an intense level. We walked for hours, praising the Lord and trying to understand what it all meant. I remember clearly that at one point, we sat down beside the Truckee River which runs through downtown Reno. We were in a park which was almost deserted except for a flock of wild ducks which landed in the water. I felt God's love pouring through me and out to everything around me.

We just sat there silently, feeling God's love all around us and rejoicing. Some of the ducks came up out of the water and waddled over to us. I felt such love for them, as I had never felt before, and I had always loved animals. Some of them just sat down beside us for a while. We didn't say a word, but each of us knew what the other was feeling, so we simply smiled. This experience lasted for several hours, and then slowly faded away. When it was gone, I really felt desolate. How could I be that close to God more of the time? I knew it was totally His doing when it happened, but what did I have to do to bring myself to the place where He would be that close and that available more of the time? I was very confused.

That evening the entire group decided that since we could not get home until Sunday anyway, we might as well spend a few dollars and take a bus to San Francisco, particularly since the others had never been there before. We pooled our money and set out for San Francisco, arriving there late on Saturday morning. Dennis and I continued to be filled with thoughts of our experience, and we were both extremely anxious to understand what it all meant.

We all decided to break into two small groups and walk around the city. The two women who were with us tired fairly early in the evening and went back to the motel, but Dennis and I continued to walk. Because it was getting late, we walked into the North Beach section of the city. By then we were beginning to get tired of walking, so we went into one of the coffeehouses. There was a girl who was singing folk music on a small stage. When we sat down, she began singing "Amazing Grace," and the words and music touched me in a deeper way than ever before. It bothered me that I simply could not understand what it really meant. It left me feeling terribly wistful. What was I supposed to do? I just couldn't understand what all of this meant. We walked late into the night trying to figure it all out.

As the time passed, I became more and more confused. I felt that our experience had been given to us for a definite purpose, and that it called for some kind of action on our part. The problem was that I could not discern what that course of action was supposed to be. At the time, I was ready to give up everything if only I could find out what God wanted me to do. When we finally got back to where we were staying, at about three o'clock in the morning, I tried to sleep, but by five o'clock I was still wide awake. The other women in my room were sound asleep, so I went to the office of the motel to find out where the nearest Episcopal church was. Leaving a message for the others, I set off to attend the seven o'clock service.

The morning was clear and beautiful. I boarded a cable car that took me to the church. When I arrived, I found that it was one of the largest churches I had ever seen. There were flights of stairs leading to the front door. As I entered, I was amazed at the beauty of the interior. I found that the early service was to be held in a small chapel, off to the side of the main sanctuary. The communion service was lovely, and I again felt that God was very near. But I also continued to feel that I was missing some key in my understanding.

It was Palm Sunday, the day which commemorates Jesus' entrance into Jerusalem, and I felt like many of the people in that first Palm Sunday crowd must have felt. I knew of the glory of Jesus Christ, but I felt deeply that my understanding of the truth about what really was going on, and the truth about what happened after, was sorely lacking. I had read the accounts in the synoptic gospels, but I felt I had a big block to understanding with my heart. I remember looking around almost frantically, searching for someone who would somehow know of my dilemma and answer all my questions. I felt as if a miracle were about to happen.

But nothing happened. I walked out of the church more confused and tied up inside than when I had entered. Seating myself on the stairs of the church and looking out across the bay, I began sobbing as if I would never stop. After a while the rest of my group came along wanting some breakfast, so we walked toward Fisherman's Wharf. I just couldn't eat, so I excused myself and promised to meet them at an appointed time. However, it seemed as if I was being pulled to the little beach at the edge of the park in front of Gheridelli Square. The day was chilly, but I took off my shoes and waded in the water. My mind was in a turmoil. Was I supposed to leave everything, and go in search of this knowledge which seemed just out of my reach? I seated myself in the sand, and as I sat there, a young man approached me. He sat down and said, "You look like you are having trouble. Do you need someone to talk to?" Gratefully I poured out all that was troubling me. He said that he had been searching for a deeper knowledge of God, too, but that he had been using a lot of acid (LSD) to aid him. He gave me his name and address and promised that if I decided to come back, he would help me find a job and a place to stay.

When he walked away, I knew two things. First, whatever I did, I had to go home and resolve difficulties there first. There had never been any question whatsoever that wherever I was, Joshua would be with me. He had been given to me as a precious gift, and it was that gift which had really led me back to God. Secondly, my relationship with my husband had never been right, and I was full of bitterness and anger. Yet, I knew I had the responsibility to go back and see what God led me to do.

I cried all the way home on the plane, for I felt that as I left San Francisco, I was leaving that sense of an imminent miracle behind also.

Upon my arrival home, my husband sensed that something major had happened, yet as hard as I tried, I could not make him understand what it was. He had always disdained my search for God, and could not comprehend what was going on inside of me. I told him that I could not take the hurt of our relationship anymore, and that changes had to occur if we were to go on. We agreed to try really hard for a year, and then to take stock again.

Things seemed to take a turn for the better in our home life, but my spiritual struggles were just beginning. The apparent futility of my search began closing in around me, and as a kind of last resort, I decided that I might learn something from a heavier drug experience. I had smoked quite a bit of marijuana, but I decided it was time to see what could be learned from an experience on acid. I must admit, it was rather a disappointment from the point of view of gaining any insight. I tried it several times, but always found myself with a resultant letdown. The only insight I seemed to get from it was the knowledge that I was embarking upon something very dangerous. And as it turned out, my final experience with the drug was terribly frightening. I had the feeling that someone or something was trying to take over my body. I became nauseated and kept almost falling asleep, which was not a typical reaction to the drug at all. Yet I felt that if I let myself fall asleep, this thing, whatever it was, would take over. That was the end of my search through drugs.

I began turning to Eastern philosophies and religions. I started reading *Be Here Now* by Baba Ram Dass. The mysticism of it struck a responsive chord in my own experience, but I felt it was off the track in an indescribable way. I continued to feel that the closeness I had felt to God was tied up with some type of mystic experience, but I was completely lost as to where to turn to find the source.

As a result of a talk with a friend who was involved

with Transcendental Meditation, I became very interested in searching that avenue for a clue. I went through the training, and practiced the technique faithfully. Physically, it seemed to have a good effect, in that my terrible nervousness was calmed. However, as far as finding any answers to my quest for God, I was terribly disappointed. The god which they seemed to be pursuing was a kind of hazy, undefined force, not anything like the strong personality of love and peace and power I had experienced. I continued to practice the technique, however, as a kind of tranquilizer.

At this time I was led to a study of the synoptic gospels. I began reading them with a totally new understanding, and Jesus became a real person for me. My love for Him grew tremendously. For example, I began to experience the stories of the Bible instead of just reading about what had happened, and the excitement mounted as the parables took on new meaning. It was as if someone had opened my eyes; yet, I could not seem to grasp how everything fit together. I was beginning to experience the tremendously gentle love of Jesus, but it was impossible for me to see how everything was to be applied to my life. I had recently read Matthew and a few chapters in Mark when I made a decision which was to change my whole life. Specifically, I had left college at the end of my junior year, and because of my teaching job, felt it would be of great benefit to return and obtain my degree. I therefore enrolled in summer school at the University of Wyoming, forty miles away.

This decision changed the course of my life in a way I could never have imagined.

## 2

# *The Advent of Darkness*

Summer school was to start soon. I made the decision to attend. I made all the necessary arrangements, ensuring that Joshua would be taken care of while I was gone during the day, finding a car pool to participate in, getting supplies and finalizing all the other details which needed to be accomplished.

I remember distinctly the day I drove alone to Laramie to register. As I parked near the campus, I had the very strong sensation that something significant was about to happen. The feeling was not the same as what I had experienced in San Francisco, of a miracle being imminent. I simply sensed that something big was approaching.

My class work took all of the time I could spare. As a result, my Bible reading came to an abrupt halt. I was incredibly busy, and things were going very well at school. I was taking two literature classes, but because of my job and the fact that I was a senior, I had also been able to get into a graduate class on group leadership.

One day, about halfway into the semester, I ran out of the education building and toward the parking lot. As I hurried along I was stopped by a young man. I learned he was a member of the International Society for Krishna Consciousness (Hare Krishna). We talked for a few moments and I asked him some questions; his responses convinced me that this was definitely not what I was looking for. His god was most certainly not the loving, living Father I knew.

During the next few weeks I was approached by several other groups, but all of them left me with a sense of too many unanswered questions, or the feeling that they were just completely off the track—as I felt my Hare Krishna friend was. One afternoon this same young man stopped me and said, "I'm not going to attempt to proselytize you, but I feel that you are about to meet your guru. I just wanted to let you know what I felt." The tension was mounting, and each day my sense of expectation was growing.

On another afternoon soon after, as I hurried across the campus to meet the other women in my car pool, I realized I had forgotten my purse. I turned around and ran back across campus to retrieve it. There was a light, refreshing rain, and I marveled at the beauty around me. Returning to the parking lot, I passed the student union, and as I hurried past, a girl came out of the door with a handful of pamphlets. I looked straight at her, and she smiled at me. I had become accustomed to studying people's eyes to see if there was a spiritual feeling to them. It's difficult to explain, but it seemed that those people who were involved in spiritual matters had a liveliness in their eyes that others did not possess. At the time, however, I could not discern whether that spiritual influence was good or evil.

As I looked into this girl's eyes, I could immediately see that there was much going on within her. She approached me and asked if we could talk but much to my disappointment, I had to decline, explaining that I was about to miss my ride. She then handed me one of her pamphlets and said that she hoped I could attend one of the workshops conducted by the group she represented.

As I rode home I read and reread the pamphlet. It sounded very interesting, but I sensed there was something strange about the whole thing. Specifically, the material I read made me feel very uneasy, yet my intellectual curiosity was aroused. The pamphlet described the group, and the workshops which were held on weekends in Denver. I knew it would be impossible for me to go away for a weekend because of my busy schedule. But it went on to describe "a new prophet for a new age" who had come from Korea to share many new truths which had been given to him by God. These truths, it stated, could solve the terrible problems which plagued the world and further, this man had been given the keys to bringing love and brotherhood to the world. "There is hope," it stated. As proof of this claim, the pamphlet included pictures of a group of young people who were learning, singing, laughing, and sitting together in what appeared to be total love and harmony.

All of these things intrigued me very much, but because I knew I could not attend a weekend workshop, and because somehow it all made me feel uneasy, I put the booklet in a drawer at home and forgot about it.

Two weeks later I was studying in one of the lounges in the student union. As I was sitting there, I became aware of a clean-cut, pleasant-looking young man standing at the door. He was looking around the room as if he were searching for someone special. Taking me completely by surprise, he walked over and sat down beside me, smiling and saying something to the effect that I looked as if I were searching for something in my life. Well, as you can imagine, this caught my attention instantly!

As we talked, I found that he was with a group of young people who were traveling across the country, checking on other young people who had recently pioneered centers for their group. He further mentioned that he was involved with a national group which was trying to make the world a better place. This was, of course, a matter which was close to my heart, and I told him I was interested in hearing more about what his group actually believed. He responded that he had a series of lectures which would describe in detail exactly what the group believed.

He asked me if I would like to hear the first presentation. As we walked I said, "Before we start, I need to know one thing. Does your group believe the Second Coming of Christ is imminent?" This question had been on my heart very much in recent weeks.

He looked at me quizzically and responded, "We think so." But then he changed the subject quickly. His answer, though, was enough to hold my interest.

We sat on the lawn and he started the lecture, which turned out to be a long, detailed—and supposedly scientific—explanation of who God really is. It asserted, among other things, that the creation was a reflection of God in the same way that a painting is a reflection of the artist. Therefore, because one is able to discern facets of the artist's character from his painting, similarly one can tell things about God's character from studying His creation. The lecture then proceeded to analyze certain chosen characteristics in the creation to prove that God has dual characteristics of male and female, positive and negative, inner essence and outer form. The lecture also included many other subjects which seemed a bit contrived and strange. But I had to admit that it sounded reasonable. Yet, I had much to learn about God's attitude concerning man's ability to reason, and the difficulties it can get him into if he tries to do things on his own through his own powers and philosophies.

When the lecture was over, I felt a strange combination of enthusiasm and apprehension. The thoughts and concepts I had heard challenged me intellectually. For example, my years of growing up had been filled with books, and I had a real passion for reading and studying history and literature. As a result of this background, I was intellectually interested in what I had heard; however, I had the feeling that something was wrong, a kind of undefined uneasiness. The young man pressed me to set a time to hear the second lecture. I was hesitant, yet I had been searching for answers for so long that I had to consider the possibility that he might have what I had been looking for so frenetically. So we determined the time and place for the next day.

When I arrived at the appointed place on the following day, I discovered that the young man's bus team was leaving earlier than they had originally planned. I felt somewhat relieved, but he quickly assured me that I could hear the same lectures from a girl who was living in Laramie. He had already arranged a time for me, and I felt I could not find a graceful way to decline. It was very difficult for me to say no to people if my doing so seemed to hurt their feelings, and of course, my hesitancy appeared to cause him great distress. When the time came, I did not want to go, but I truly felt that it would be very rude not to appear, so I kept the appointment.

Somewhat to my surprise, although by then I had suspected it, the girl was the same girl I had met a few days earlier coming out of the student union. We sat on the lawn, visited for a few minutes, and resumed the lectures. The material in the second lecture was similar to what I had heard in the first lecture. She spoke of the family unit as being the basic unit created by God for man. This appealed to me greatly, and I tried to pay attention as she explained how God, a man, his wife and their children were originally intended to form a "four-position foundation" which is supposedly the fulfillment of God's goodness, and the ultimate reason for creation. This "four-position foundation" is also alleged to be the means through which God's power is channeled to flow out to all of His creation, in order that it may even exist. Because of this, the creation of the "four-position foundation" is intended to be the ultimate purpose for the entire creation. This theory could supposedly be substantiated by another rather long, involved theory which, when standing by itself, seemed totally logical. However, I was to learn later that because a theory appears logical within itself, it does not prove it is true.

When the lecture was over, I was once again left with a terrible feeling of uneasiness, yet, as before, I could not dispute the logic of the theory as it stood by itself. I decided not to judge anything until I heard the entire presentation. The ideas themselves seemed kind of exciting.

We talked further and I found out that the girl's name was Mary, and that she was a member of the Unification Church, of which I had never heard before. This was the summer of 1972, when the organization had little, if any, publicity, especially in Wyoming. I liked Mary and did not resist her attempt to arrange a meeting for me to hear the third lecture.

The day on which she presented the third lecture was a refreshing, sunlit day, and I felt good to be alive. I met her on the lawn again and with great gusto she launched into the lecture almost immediately. At that point something strange happened: I felt a great rebellion toward what she was teaching. The lecture was on the original fall of man, and it had the same effect on me as my reading of the Greek myths had had. She was telling me that Lucifer, one of God's archangels, had been with Adam and Eve in the Garden of Eden. Adam and Eve had not grown to maturity yet, Mary told me, when, through some circumstances which were not all Lucifer's fault, not all Eve's fault, nor even totally Adam's fault, Lucifer seduced Eve, who later seduced Adam. This constituted a spiritual fall first, and second, a physical fall. To me, the whole story appeared to be a strange and fantastic myth. I was not wholly unacquainted with the theory that the fall of man had been a sexual fall, but this interpretation put my spirit into a total state of resistance. I had always felt that this was a stupid reason for man to go against God. Yet, later as I thought about it, I felt I had done much the same kind of thing when I had chosen my husband over God. And I also had the feeling that my actions had caused me terrible suffering. I was still bearing tremendous guilt, even though I had asked for God's forgiveness. Mary sensed my reaction and begged me to just put aside my feelings until I heard the whole lecture series. Then, she added, I could look at the entire presentation in a logical way. I agreed to do this, but had the feeling that I was on the wrong track again.

When we met next, I had an even more violent reaction to Mary and what she taught me. The fourth lecture pertained to Jesus. Before we even started, I was overcome by something which I could not understand, and as we sat down on the lawn, my whole being was in revulsion against Mary. I actually became nauseated at the sight of her. My reaction to this situation was one of terrible embarrassment and consternation, and when I tried to analyze it from a logical point of view, I discovered there was nothing logical about it. Because I could not analyze it, I simply let go and let myself experience the revulsion. Then very clearly, these words came to me, "This is evil!" and I had the strong compulsion to run away.

"Now wait a minute," I said to myself, "what has she ever done to make me feel this way? Nothing. This just is not logical, so I'd better ignore it, and perhaps these negative feelings will go away before I hurt her feelings."

It took all the will power I had to sit there and politely listen to what she said. First she showed me a booklet that dealt with the "Divine Principle" (the philosophy she was teaching me) and its relationship to economics. I was not impressed, primarily because I was constantly fighting nausea. She then began the teaching, and as I listened, I became more and more appalled—and then more and more angry.

As the lecture progressed, Mary told me that Jesus did not exist before His birth, but that because His ancestors had paid enough indemnity (suffering in payment for sin), He was able to be born sinless. She further stated that Jesus was supposed to establish the kingdom of heaven on earth during His lifetime, but because of the disbelief of the Jews, He was crucified, and all God's plans were foiled. This is a very simplistic explanation of the whole lecture, but it emphasizes the basic points. By the time she had finished, I was so insulted that I jumped up to leave because I felt she had really slandered Jesus. It is difficult to explain, but at that time I felt I belonged to Jesus and He belonged to me. I loved Him very much (from afar, in that I did not at that time have a personal relationship with Him). He had touched me during that time of intense Bible reading just before I began summer school.

I had not read enough Scripture to be able to refute what Mary told me, but I sensed it was all contrived. I was in tears and walked away with her following me and talking the whole time. I was not very aware of what she said, as I headed for the nearest building to find the restroom so I could wash my face and regain control of my emotions. Mary followed me into the building. "I know how you feel," she said, "and I felt the same way the first time I heard this. You know, I was raised a Catholic, and I love Jesus very much. You just have to hear the rest of the lectures to understand how it all fits together." I believe she tried to set up another time for us to meet, but I would not commit myself.

Several weeks passed, my calm returned, and I didn't dwell very much on what had happened. My classes were going very well, and I was enjoying them very much. I met several new friends, including a girl named Margaret, who was also in the education program and about to graduate. In addition, in my group leadership class, which was given as part of the Adult Education program, I met a man who was about to get his doctorate in school administration. And there were several others who were in the education program with whom I had become friends. We all agreed that we did not want to be tied to the public school system, and were beginning to talk about the possibility of starting a free school in Cheyenne. This project took up most of my open time.

At the same time I was also trying to get into a pilot program for student teaching and taking classes in Cheyenne at the extension office for fall semester. Since this program appeared to be the only plausible way for me to be able to do my student teaching, I was very anxious to get into it. Just as the semester was about to end, I was again approached by Mary, who had been following me doggedly, and she proposed that I hear the end of the lecture series. She reasoned that I had already heard most of the material, and it would be a shame not to listen to it all before I made a judgment. Now I really did like Mary, despite the episode with the nausea, and did not want to disappoint her, so I agreed. It turned out that Margaret had already heard as much as I had, so we were to come to the center to hear the rest on an afternoon which we both had free.

We met Mary at the house which she was renting for the organization, and as we walked through the front door, I sensed an atmosphere which was totally foreign to me. It made me uneasy, yet I was very curious. As we went into a back room to hear the lectures, I noticed that the room was bare, as was most of the house. As Mary launched into a long, detailed lecture on Bible history (which I recently discovered was full of inaccuracies), I found my interest failing. As we sat there, I became aware of a growing pain in the pit of my stomach. Before long I could not even sit up straight; the pain was so overwhelming, I had to lie on the floor to be able to bear it. The history lectures seemed to drag on forever, but in the end, she had, with the aid of the inaccurate figures, drawn a parallel between the times from Jacob, who she had taught was the first man to fulfill certain conditions set by God and Jesus, and the time from Jesus' death until now.

This entire, elaborate presentation was supposed to prove that the new messiah had been born between the years of 1917 and 1930 and was at that very moment trying to establish the kingdom of heaven on earth, something which Jesus had not been allowed to accomplish. Now this caught my attention, since I had been convinced that the Second Coming was to take place soon. Having never read the appropriate chapters of Revelation from the Bible, I had a very hazy concept of how this was supposed to take place, so that because of the elaborate explanation which she had just given me, this whole theory seemed logical. I was terribly excited, yet the pain was growing worse.

Mary proceeded to give me a rather contrived explanation as to why this new messiah would be born in Korea, but I think that I wanted so much for my search to be ended that I wanted to believe she was really proving something. She had recently told me that the man in charge of the church was a Korean named Sun Myung Moon. Earlier that day, I had noticed one of the rooms which appeared to be a prayer room, and on a table in that room I had seen a picture of a Korean man whom I suspected to be Moon. After all these details had raced through my mind, I asked, "Is Sun Myung Moon the new messiah?" Mary just smiled but said nothing. I was in a turmoil, as the pain grew suddenly much worse. Margaret was furious and wanted to hear no more, although I don't believe she was a Christian; in fact, I don't remember her being at all religious.

By then I could hardly bear the pain anymore, and Mary offered to take me to meet my ride. As we drove back to the university parking lot, she told me several things. First of all, I told her that I suspected I was pregnant with my second child. "No," she said, "I don't feel like you are, and I'm hardly ever wrong about these things." I thought that she did not know what she was talking about. She then said something very strange. "You'd better think and pray about what you've heard, because I can promise you that if you don't, it will haunt you the rest of your life!" I met my ride, and was severely ill all the way home; in fact, I was so sick that I had to be in bed for nearly three days.

The next week was final examination week, and I only saw Mary once or twice in passing. On one of these occasions she showed me a picture of Sun Myung Moon and his wife, who she referred to as being the "true parents" of mankind. After this encounter I saw her no more for quite awhile, since I had no reason to come to Laramie after summer school had ended.

I was notified during final exam week that I had been accepted into the pilot program for student teaching in Cheyenne, and I was delighted. My life was very busy with preparations for the coming semester, including arranging for Joshua to stay with my mother-in-law, whom I really loved, while I attended classes. Before I knew it, I was in the middle of school again. The first half of the semester was spent sitting in on English classes in all the secondary schools in

Cheyenne during the mornings and attending education classes in the afternoons. During this time, I found it necessary to leave my job at the Adult Learning Center. As the second half of the semester approached, we were to pick three teachers whose classes we had visited as our choices for supervising teachers during our student teaching. I had a very fortunate chance to sit in on a seventh grade remedial English skills class at a school near my home. The school had a reputation for being the roughest and worst junior high in Cheyenne, but I loved it. The teacher, Mrs. Martin, was a wonderful, warmhearted person, who did wonders with the children in her program. I had had experience assisting in remedial reading classes for the summer school program in my home town and felt a great desire to work in the field. I loved working with the children, and felt a great fulfillment at being able to help them. As a result, I was able to do my student teaching there, and an added advantage was that it was within walking distance of my house, and we had only one car. I enjoyed this teaching experience tremendously, and really wanted to finish school so I could go into the remedial field.

During my student teaching experience, several events occurred which were to change my circumstances completely. First of all, my suspicions about being pregnant were confirmed. Secondly, my husband was offered a very good job in Rawlins, which was about 130 miles away.

At this particular time our marriage was even more of an empty shell than it had been the summer before, and I was in despair over the entire situation. I had not wanted to bring another life into a marriage as troubled as ours. But from the moment I knew there was a new life within me, I loved it with all I was.

Sometime in late November or early December, my husband moved to Rawlins, while I stayed in Cheyenne to finish my student teaching. Immediately following Thanksgiving, Joshua contracted a terrible earache. The doctor gave him one shot, and when that didn't clear it up, he would take no further action and Josh kept getting sicker. I had a serious case of bronchitis myself and was feeling a terrible depression. I was also very lonely after my student teaching weeks were over, and I remembered what Mary had told me. She had also predicted that if I didn't do something about what I had heard, I would go into a deep depression. All these things, plus the fact that I just liked Mary so much, led me to ask my brother-in-law, who was attending school in Laramie, to try to find her and tell her I needed to see her.

My mind became filled with thoughts of what I had heard the past summer. The prospects of my finishing school were growing quite dim, because we would be ninety miles away from the university instead of forty. I also had to admit to myself that I was much happier and at peace when my husband was gone than when he was at home. It seemed that the only bright spot in my life was Joshua.

A week passed before Mary contacted me and said she was going to drive over to Cheyenne—I was delighted at the prospect of having someone to talk to.

During this period I had continued to attend the Episcopal church, but I had not yet heard anything which refuted the teachings I had been given by Mary. In fact, as I said before, the Scriptures were hardly ever discussed. And still I was plagued by the feeling that there was something God wanted me to do. I had always wanted desperately to do something which would help the world become a better place. So when Mary showed up at the front door, I was open to almost anything she could have said.

I discovered that she had been in an automobile accident shortly after I had seen her the last time, and had to return to the Chicago area to recuperate for a couple of months; she had just returned to Wyoming recently. We talked for quite awhile, and she shared with me that one young man had joined the church since I had seen her, so she had acquired her first member in Wyoming. Before the afternoon was over she was to have her second. Just before they left, she asked me if I wanted to sign a paper for membership. I had no idea of what the ramifications of my joining would be. It did not even occur to me that I would ever move into a center, so I signed.

## 3

# *Caught in the Maelstrom*

It was not more than a week after I became a member of the Unification Church that we moved to Rawlins. I was both excited and very upset by the move. There was hope in the fact that my husband had secured a job which interested him very much, and which would help us to improve our adverse financial condition. I felt that perhaps these new circumstances might give us a fresh start in our marriage. Yet, it also seemed we were simply cut off from the world, because the closest town was about ninety miles away, and we knew no one in Rawlins. In past situations, the tension had always been eased by the nearly continual presence of one or more of our friends in our home, but now we were faced with only each other.

An additional complication was that I was experiencing an extremely difficult pregnancy. Somehow, I had developed an allergic reaction to the pregnancy itself. In addition, my sinuses were blocked and I was having severe bronchial problems. As a result, I could not sleep many nights and spent much of my time sitting on the couch in the living room.

Mary was keeping in touch with me faithfully, ensuring that I always had an abundance of reading material. Also, I had purchased a book entitled *Divine Principle* the day when I had heard the last lecture, although I had already read and studied it several times. Now I was ready for some deeper material, so Mary provided me with a number of copies of speeches which had been presented by Sun Myung Moon and which were known collectively as "Master Speaks."

As I became more familiar with the ideas of the "Principle," Mary explained her interpretation of the strange events which had occurred during the time when I heard the lectures. It was, she explained, a question of indemnity. That is, the nausea I experienced and the pains in my stomach were all payment for my hearing the "truth." That seemed logical to me at the time, although she admitted that she had never heard of anyone else having such a severe reaction. She stated that God must want me very much for Satan to go to the trouble of exacting so much indemnity in payment for my hearing the "Principle." This logic was, of course, very complimentary.

As I read the "Master Speaks" I became very inspired, although there were things in the speeches that really made me cringe. However, I believed that these things were simply concepts I would have to understand more deeply. I had always been very idealistic, and Moon's talk of our responsibility to go out and work to save the world appealed to me greatly. I thought of a time when I had been in high school taking a contemporary world problems class. We had had a lecture one day on the plight of the Asian people, particularly the Vietnamese. The teacher had spoken of the terrible oppression which these people had experienced for thousands of years; hearing this was almost more than I could bear. After school, I had gone home with the plight of the millions of starving, oppressed, even tortured people in the world weighing heavily on my heart. I cried for hours and could not even bring myself to eat. My mother, who is a gentle and dear person, sat me down and told me that I must stop torturing myself over something about which I could do nothing. I knew she was right, but my heart cried out in anger and pain that it had to be that way. Because of these feelings which I always carried within me, I yearned to go out into the world and do all I could to correct the problems. My enthusiasm for Moon was growing rapidly.

However, it was about this time that additional strange things began happening to me, mostly at night while I was awake with my physical problems. I became aware that I was not alone in the room, which undoubtedly will sound utterly unbelievable to anyone who has never been aware of the spiritual phenomena around us. However, in the past few years I have experienced dozens of such manifestations.

On those nights as I sat alone, the room would become filled with terror and I could hardly make myself sit still. I had been taught by the "Principle" that there were always good and evil spiritual beings around us everywhere and that the spirits of the dead, especially our ancestors, were with us all the time. I did not know at that point that the Bible teaches we are never to have any recourse with the spirits of the dead under any circumstances: "If man has recourse to the spirits of the dead or to magicians, to prostitute himself by following them, I shall set my face against that man and outlaw him from his people" (Lev. 20:6, Jerusalem). And again in verse 27 of the same chapter, "Any man or woman who is a necromancer or magician must be put to death by stoning; their blood shall be on their own heads." In short, I had no idea that my voyage into the world of the spirits was considered a grave sin by my Father in heaven. In fact there were many things which I was to engage in which were considered sins in the Bible, but then, I had never really read the Bible, so I had no protection.

I began to feel that the entire atmosphere of my life was dark. Yet, as I said before, I had no discernment as to whether the spiritual powers surrounding me were of God or Satan. Satan, as I was later to find out, is indeed the great deceiver. For example, it is easy enough to identify his works when they are accompanied by a feeling of terror, but his most dangerous influences are accompanied by the feeling that one is being led in the right direction. Only the Bible can tell us the things which are of God and those which are not.

In summary, I believed that everything was falling apart in my life. My marriage was becoming increasingly disagreeable, with nearly every day punctuated by words of anger and resentment. There were many nights when our only conversations were held in loud and angry tones, and I began to have the feeling at the time that I was living in the middle of a soap opera.

Our marriage was becoming more and more unbearable for me, especially since I had grown up with a tremendous dislike for any kind of violence or yelling. Unfortunately, as nearly as I could determine, there was no remedy for the situation. I had read just enough Scripture to know that divorce was not allowed by the Lord, so I resigned myself to living out a loveless marriage as payment for the sin of choosing my husband over God. This was especially painful as I was about to bring another life into the world. I did have some comforts at that time, though: my enjoyment of Joshua, my anticipation of the baby's birth, and the fact that I truly enjoyed our new house. However, I was beginning to notice that Joshua was being affected quite negatively by the tense atmosphere in the house whenever my husband was home. I was very nervous most of the time, waiting for the next blowup between us.

On April 4, 1973, my daughter was born. I named her Julie (in remembrance of an infant sister who had died just before she was born from an RH factor problem) Elizabeth (because the name means "consecrated to God"). Julie Beth was absolutely beautiful; she had bright red hair and the sweetest disposition in the world, I thought.

Shortly after Julie Beth was born, Mary came to Rawlins to visit for a weekend. My mother had stayed with us for a week after the baby's arrival, but she had to return home just prior to Mary's visit. So it was such a joy to see Mary again, primarily because I had been terribly lonely since our move. The other young couples whom we had met passed their time drinking and committing adultery. Obviously neither of these things held the slightest appeal for me; indeed I had an extremely strong sense of morals to which the Moon doctrine greatly appealed, because according to this doctrine, the greatest sin possible was a sexual sin. My own feelings were in total agreement with this concept.

Mary and I had long and deep discussions while she was visiting, and I was greatly inspired to begin working for the Unification Church. We talked of the possibility of my witnessing there in Rawlins and getting the people whom I was able to contact to Laramie for the lectures. I was very excited at the prospect of finally being able to do something worthwhile with my life again.

During this visit and later visits, Mary taught the

"Principle" to my husband. The only effect this appeared to have was to make him more and more hostile. He had felt for a long time that my search for God was threatening him, and this new turn of events made him absolutely furious. The terrible screaming increased, and I became increasingly determined to pursue my own personal beliefs.

After approximately a month of this stalemate, we decided that I should finish school so that I could teach and hopefully find some fulfillment in that. It was actually my husband who suggested that I might be able to stay with Mary for the summer while I attended some classes, an idea which excited me very much. I could acquire academic hours toward my degree, while at the same time I could work for the church. Mary agreed very readily. In retrospect, I can see that I was terribly naive and certainly had no idea about what I was getting into.

It was determined that I should move into the Unification Church center the weekend before I was to register for school. I knew another married girl who also had two children and who lived in Laramie, and she and I decided to take turns caring for the children. My classes were in the morning so I would be on campus all morning witnessing when I was not in class, and after lunch I would walk to the other girl's house, where the children would be, and I would care for the children while she went to campus to witness. The whole situation seemed very agreeable.

I put together the clothes I would need for the summer and prepared to go to Laramie. The agreement was that I would, as far as I could see, return to Rawlins when summer school ended. During this time my husband and I had been attending the Episcopal church in

Rawlins. This was the first time he had ever accompanied me to church and, I must admit, I was suspicious of his motives, rightfully or not. The day before we were to go to Laramie, I was in the house busily getting clothes ready. Suddenly the doorbell rang, my husband answered it, and then without a word, he left. I went to the window just in time to see him get into a car with the local Episcopal priest and his wife. As they sat in the car in front of our house for nearly an hour talking in secret, I became incredibly indignant. If they had something to say about what I was doing, why didn't they come in and discuss it with me? At that point, if someone had taken the Scriptures and pointed out the places which absolutely disprove the Moon doctrines, of which there are many, I would have been very open. I still had personal doubts about some of the beliefs; however, the "Principle" quoted the Bible to prove many of its teachings, and I had no reason to disbelieve what they taught. It was much later when I discovered that most of the quotes they use are taken completely out of context and that they are distorted in interpretation to prove anything Moon wants to prove. I was also appalled later to find out that many of the Scriptures which I had used to prove the "Principle," when read in full, actually disprove the teachings.

Now, I had always been a firm believer in speaking openly to individuals about any differences which might prevail between them and myself. Thus, I felt that what my husband, the priest and his wife were doing was dishonest, furtive, and just plain rude. While I was enduring what I felt to be a supreme insult, there was another knock at the door. To my great joy, it was several members of the "family," a term used by members of the Unification Church to refer to themselves.

I was so relieved to see someone who I felt was "with me" instead of "against me" that I broke down in tears.

Among other things, they explained to me that Satan would do everything in his power to keep me from working for Moon; and my husband, the priest and his wife's behavior at this time appeared to me to be so clearly motivated by evil that I readily accepted their explanation. By the time they left, I was feeling even more indignation than before, and it was at this point that the priest's wife came to the door. I invited her in, and she proceeded to beg me not to go into this den of iniquity for the summer. She told me that she knew what kinds of things went on in these places, that there was free sex and all manner of immorality. As she begged me not to commit adultery, I regarded it as a pitiable situation of ignorance on her part, because I had absolutely no intention of committing adultery. Considering the beliefs and practices of the Unification Church, which does not ever permit men and women to be in the same room alone together, or touch in any way, this was the most absurd accusation she could have made. Besides, at that point, I felt that sexual matters had been the cause of all my woes, and I did not care if I lived the rest of my life in a celibate state. So, you can imagine my indignant fury at hearing those allegations! "It just has to be Satan," I remember thinking. With every bit of control I could muster, I calmly assured her that committing adultery was the least of my intentions, and in fact, was not even in the realm of possibility and I then asked her to leave.

I was absolutely furious with them for their ignorance, for not attempting to find out what it was that I really believed, and especially at my husband for allowing it to happen, since he had heard the teachings on the subject. I know now that what occurred was a tragic lack of communication and, as I look back to that event, I just have to praise the Lord for the power of forgiveness and understanding which He gives as a free gift to me now.

The next morning we packed all of our things and headed for Laramie. When we arrived at the center, everyone greeted us with great enthusiasm. The house we were to live in was quite large, and we were given a room downstairs with the other girls. By then there were six or eight people in the center, including several people from other parts of the country who had been sent to the center. Two were from Wyoming. I must admit I was suddenly afraid; the house felt cold and lonely to me, and I was overcome with a vague fear. Yet, everyone acted so warmly that I thought it must be my own imagination. But, as my husband drove off that evening, I began crying, because I knew instinctively that my life was about to change inalterably.

The next morning was Sunday. We were awakened at five o'clock for a weekly prayer service. Everyone met in front of a small table with candles and a large picture of Moon and his wife, the "true parents." We prayed and sang, and I knew that this was supposed to be a time of great closeness to my Father in heaven. But I kept feeling that something was missing; I simply did not have that overpowering sense of God's presence that I used to get at communion services. But, I overcame this feeling by concluding that there must be something wrong with me.

The customs of the house were new and strange to me. For example, each minute was scheduled and planned. All of the household chores were taken care of early in the morning, leaving the great bulk of the day for witnessing and selling all manner of things, ranging from candles to cookbooks, door-to-door, and attending "Principle" lectures with the people we had met and who would come with us.

The arrangement with the other young mother worked out quite satisfactorily, and my days were a comfortable combination of action and being with the children. I was quite contented; in fact, it was somewhat disturbing that I enjoyed being on my own, away from my husband, as much as I did. I began acquiring a better sense of my self again, and it had been years since I had experienced that. Also, I found myself with a growing attachment to the other people in the center, primarily because living that closely and working so zealously for a common cause nurtures this feeling to a great extent. There was, because of Mary, and not because of the doctrine, much loving and caring in the house. Specifically, this was the only time in my experience in the Moonies when there was true caring for each other with no ulterior motive present, and where the caring was not used only to manipulate the members. I believe Mary brought her compassion into the cult and that it had just not been snuffed out yet!

As the weeks passed, these feelings must have been apparent to my husband when he came to visit on the weekends, because the friction between us came to a real crisis point. I was beginning to realize that our basic natures were at complete odds with one another. Another factor was that I had spoken to Mary, who in turn had spoken to several of her superiors, and even to Moon himself, and the decision was that when a married person joined the "family," that person had a responsibility to have the "Principle" taught to his or her mate. If, however, the mate refused to accept the teachings, and would not let the member work for Moon, then it was permissible for the person who was a member to leave the uncooperative mate. Upon leaving, however, the member still had a seven-year responsibility to try to convert the mate, even if the only channel left open was through prayer. This new light on my situation was not an impetus for divorce. I really don't believe they could have said anything that would have caused me to harm the marriage or to break it up, if the marriage had been happy. However, I had been extremely miserable in a marriage which was a terrible mistake in the first place. The only reason I had let things continue as they had for the past year was that I felt so strongly that God wanted me to go on because of the things I had read in the Bible. However, by this time I fully believed that Moon was God's representative, and I completely trusted whatever he said about the matter. Mary had the opportunity to ask him personally about the situation, and his opinion was that I should take the course I have described. I suppose I was also relieved to believe that there was a way out of the terrible mistake I had made in going into the marriage initially.

Several things happened within a short time which led me to change my whole life and realm of possibilities. One weekend when my husband visited, we were asked to dinner by a friend of ours who had been reading and studying tarot cards for over a year. It was not a particular surprise when she asked us if she could read the cards for us after dinner. I was very enthusiastic about it, and we both agreed. I was very aware of spiritual powers in the room, but I had no fear since I had been taught that these powers were all around anyway. In fact, I felt that if these powers could possibly confirm that I was doing the right thing, then perhaps my husband would listen and change.

Again, I was trifling with things about which I had no knowledge, and I did not know that the Bible states very clearly that under no circumstances should we ever try to discern the future by contacting spirits of the dead. The tarot card reading was a personal confirmation that I was doing the right thing. I don't remember the entire sequence of events, but the reading demonstrated very definitely that I should pursue the course upon which I had embarked, and made some rather pointed threats against my husband should he refuse to go with me into the Moonies. Now, the girl reading the cards had absolutely no reason to want us in the Moonies; in fact, she was against the idea. However, the powers of darkness with whom we were dealing had every reason in the world to lead me astray, but at the time, I thought that if the spirits said something, it had to be true. In other words I felt very strongly that this was the confirmation for which I had been looking.

Soon after, my husband and I had a serious argument, one of the worst ever. We had agreed to go to Cheyenne on the following weekend for the children to see his grandparents, but as a result of our argument, he would not speak one word to me from the moment he came to pick us up until we arrived in Cheyenne, and then he left immediately. I was at my wit's end, full of anger and hurt, and completely exhausted by the whole thing. When I hadn't seen him by the middle of the next morning, I called my father in Colorado to come and get us; I could not tolerate another day. He and my brother arrived the next morning, and we went back to Laramie to collect all our things. Meanwhile, I had told my husband and Mary that I was going to Colorado to straighten matters out, and then to decide whether or not to file for divorce. I still considered myself firmly entrenched in the Unification Church, but my life just had to be put in order before I could serve in the way I felt I must. I was doing exactly as I had been counseled to do by Moon and Mary in their meeting together which I described earlier. That is, I was becoming a devout convert to the Unification Church.

## 4

## *Disguised as an Angel of Light*

During the middle of the first night following my arrival at my parents' home, I awakened suddenly; terror permeated the whole room. Not more than a few seconds after I awakened, Julie Beth woke up screaming. I turned on the light, but I was still terribly frightened. I was finally able to soothe Julie and get her back to sleep, but I was so terrified that I could not sleep. This terror-filled awakening during the night was to become a frequent occurrence for me during the next couple of years.

I had been told to sing certain "family" songs and to pray when this happened, and at the center in Wyoming, Mary would sing and sprinkle what she called "holy salt" all around the house. There was a definite ritual to this sprinkling of the salt. For example, it had to be sprinkled in each corner and then in the middle of the room, and a prayer was to be said in the name of the "true parents," as were all prayers. I did not happen to have any "holy salt," so I simply sang, prayed, and read the "Principle." There was no relief, though, and after each awakening, I would finally fall asleep completely exhausted. We had been taught to expect these attacks, since we were doing God's will, and Satan would be very angry. It never occurred to me at the time that we were extremely vulnerable to Satan because we were members of the kingdom of darkness, and he had every right to annoy us and claim power over us. Never did I, nor anyone I knew, experience any real power against the spirits while I was in the Unification Church. I merely thought it was a necessary evil which had to be endured; that is, more indemnity.

Soon after my return to Colorado, I initiated a counseling relationship with a psychologist, because this was required by Colorado law before one could file for divorce. I also needed to know for certain whether there was any chance of saving my marriage. My counselor was absolutely appalled when I recounted many incidents that occurred during my marriage. He said it was undoubtedly one of the most destructive relationships he had ever encountered, and that if I insisted on continuing it, he could promise me that not only would it destroy me as a person, but it would also end up destroying the children. He added that the terrible friction between our characters would lead only to anguish.

This was a definite confirmation to me that the only possible course of action was to file for divorce. Yet, this was an incredibly painful decision, primarily because I could not face the fact that we had failed. We had married against the wishes of almost everyone I knew, and I had wanted desperately for things between us to change and work out. But here I was with what I felt to be undeniable evidence that the entire marriage was hopeless. The factor which settled the matter was the great improvement I was beginning to see in the children's dispositions, especially Joshua's. He was beginning to relax and respond to disciplinary action in a way he never had before. He was also much easier to live with, and so was I. Another factor which influenced my decision was that I had been relying quite heavily on different types of tranquilizers, except when I was pregnant and nursing my babies. I was still rather heavily dependent on them, but the dependence was slackening off. Specifically, I was going longer each day without feeling I just could not endure another minute without chemical help.

In sum, I was really beginning to relax for the first time in several years. My parents both worked, which left me at home with the children all day, and I was finding it very soothing simply to spend each day caring for Joshua and Julie and the house, and fixing the meals. I did, of course, spend at least two hours every day reading material from the Unification Church, since I was making an in-depth study of the "Principle." A new edition had recently been printed in English. Although we had been using a small, red book translated by a Korean lady named Miss Kim, we now had a new version which was much more complex, translated by another of the first missionaries to come to America from Korea, David Kim. This version was the first fully translated version of the *Divine Principle* ever to be printed in English. I read it every day, and by the time I returned to a center, I had read the entire book several times, and had made in-depth studies of most of the chapters.

My encounters with the powers of the spirit world were increasing. I was starting to have dreams which were really uncanny, and I now believe that most of these dreams were initiated by the powers of darkness, because their fruits brought nothing but evil. Other dreams I had during the same period of time I still don't understand. Approximately a month after I had gone to Colorado, I had a dream in which my husband came to me to try to convince me to return to him. In the dream, I was aware that he had another girl that he was seeing, and so I declined to come. He then smiled a very strange smile, the expression of which I had never seen on him before. Also in the dream, I was warned by several women, whom I knew were supposed to be relatives, but none of whom I recognized, that if I went back to a Unification Center, the children would be destroyed. Obviously, it was a very strange dream, and at the end of it, I ran out the door of the building where I had been, and all I could think of was that now I was (and these are the exact words), a "free spirit." When I awoke from the dream, which I did immediately, the room was filled with evil spirits. I was terrified, and could not understand what the dream meant, or what its source had been. Several days later my husband called and said that he wanted to come to Colorado to visit me and the children.

I was very upset at the prospect of his visit, because he had always been able to get me to do anything he wanted me to do, whether I wanted to or not. Consequently I was exceptionally nervous the evening he arrived. He immediately sat down and attempted to prove, using the ideas of family in the "Principle," that I should come back to him. At that point a very strange thing happened: he smiled the precise smile he had smiled in the dream. I was incredibly shocked, and sensed that I could not listen to him anymore. I made a point of staying as far away from him as possible during the remainder of his visit. I was now in complete emotional turmoil, and I reverted to taking tranquilizers.

After he left, I decided it had all been confirmation that I really could not go back to him. The dream had frightened me terribly, especially after I saw him smile that same smile, and I definitely perceived the dream as a warning. Yet, paradoxically, I felt the warning about the children was just a trick from Satan. I also was convinced that the terrible emotional turmoil which I had experienced showed that the marriage just could not continue. It was shortly after this incident that I made the positive decision to file for divorce. In retrospect, I must admit that even under the circumstances, it was a very painful and frightening decision. Indeed, up to the last moment I looked for some miracle to happen so that the marriage could survive. But I also realized that this would mean a drastic personality change on the part of him or me, and I faced the fact that this was virtually impossible for us considering the existing circumstances.

For comfort, I threw myself even more fervently into my study of "The Principle." I had also received more copies of "Master Speaks" from Mary. I read some of the teachings to my mother, and they distressed her. It was at this time that Mary stopped in to visit. She brought one of the new girls with her, and they stayed overnight. Coincidentally, my best friend was also in town, so I invited her to come over, and Mary taught her a significant portion of the "Principle." She considered it seriously and even returned to a center back in Portland, where she lived, and heard the rest of it, yet much to my dismay, she rejected it. I then looked for her life to fall apart, but to my wonderment, her situation improved and continued to do so.

I saw Mary several times during the next couple of months. She had to go to Los Angeles on selling trips on at least two occasions. Each time she came, I was more excited than before about getting back into a center. I filed for divorce that fall, and had to wait for it to become finalized before I could move back into a center. Meanwhile, Mary was searching for a center where there were other mothers with children.

In December, Mary called and told me that Moon, whom we called "Father," was coming to Denver to speak at the end of January. I was ecstatic because I wanted so much to see and hear him. It was all arranged that I could go to Denver the week preceding Moon's speech to work on the campaign. It was the most thrilling happening I could imagine.

I flew to Denver and some of the "sisters" met me at the airport. We went to the hotel where everyone was staying, and I immediately embarked upon my job assignment: handing out tickets to Moon's speech in the streets. (We had a goal for attendance which we all took very seriously.) It was a completely new revelation for me to work with such a large number of members of the Unification Church, because I had never seen more than a dozen in one place before, but now they were everywhere I turned. Many of the members from the states surrounding Colorado were present, in addition to all the members of the traveling bus team which preceded Moon in every city. These bus team members had a very polished procedure which they followed in each city where Moon was to speak. The local members would initiate the publicity, make the necessary arrangements for the place where Moon would speak, arrange accommodations for visiting members, set up a headquarters out of which all program coordination would be made, and arrange for the banquet which preceded each talk, including inviting guests to that banquet. The objective was to persuade the most prestigious and powerful guests possible to attend the banquet. When the traveling team would arrive shortly before the scheduled date for the talk, they would take charge of the entire operation. The majority of the team members would inundate the streets of the city with a tremendous publicity campaign. I personally spent the rest of that afternoon going through several large business buildings in downtown Denver, trying to give away tickets for the speech. It was extremely cold that day, but we worked steadily until the time came to meet back at our hotel for dinner. This was the routine every day until the day of the banquet, which was the day before the speech was scheduled. On this day everyone was incredibly excited because this was the day of Moon's arrival.

Whenever he came to a city, the house in which the center was located (or a special house if it was available), would be prepared for literally weeks before his arrival. Only certain selected people were allowed to work in the house toward the end, and incredible efforts were made to put the house in as near perfect shape as possible. When Moon arrived, young men were chosen as guards and placed throughout the house. There were also a few young men chosen to drive the cars and be bodyguards. Moon had one young man who traveled with him everywhere, but others were chosen in each city.

We were all so excited that we could hardly wait for the activities to begin. On the day of the speech, we performed our tasks on the streets with the most incredible zeal I had ever seen. The day went very slowly, but we did not let up for a minute. During the day I was able to spend a little time with Mary, whom I had seen very little since my arrival. We had a deep personal talk about my future. She was contacting centers all over the country, trying to find one which had other mothers with children. She discovered that there was a farm in Maryland and a center in Berkeley, California, both of which were possibilities.

We also talked about dreams, and found that we both had had many dreams about being imprisoned by the Communists for our religious beliefs. These particular dreams had troubled me greatly, because I did not feel that I would have the strength to endure any kind of tortures for my beliefs, and I could not understand where the Christian saints acquired their tremendous faith. Mary assured me that she had gone through the same type of situation and that she felt sure she could do anything for Moon now. This was a comfort to me, since I felt the necessary faith would come with time.

That evening I went to the auditorium with a great sense of anticipation, and to my amazement, I was given a seat in the center of the first row. I had built myself up to the point where I was really high, almost as if I had been using drugs. I wanted desperately to have someone who could be the recipient of my adoration, and it was very easy to adore someone I could see and hear. That night Moon gave his "Day of Hope" speech, and when he spoke of the perfect love of the perfect family, my heart melted. I had just been through a very painful divorce and the end of a very imperfect marriage, and I longed with all my heart to have a perfect family in which to raise my children. It was much later that I discovered that this talk was in theory only, because I was to see quite a few marriages which had been "blessed" by Moon himself, and not one of them even vaguely approached a perfect love. In fact many of them were just plain miserable, but my eyes were blinded to reality by the longing of my heart. At the time, though, I was absolutely ecstatic, because he even looked straight at me when he spoke of the perfect love within the perfect marriage and family. After hearing his speech, I was absolutely sure I was in the right place, doing the right thing.

It was very difficult for me to go back to my parents' home. I was terribly inspired by my experience, and wanted to get on with the work at the Unification Church immediately. In the meantime, I was delighted to be back with the children.

The next few weeks were full of anticipation. I became more and more anxious for Mary to find a center where I could take the children. During those weeks, though, I began having dreams again, and as always, I was almost continually plagued by the presence of evil. This sense of evil continued to be terrifying, but it was also becoming almost boring.

I had several dreams in which Moon appeared; these particular dreams always had a weird aura about them, but I was told by Mary that they were a real blessing. They always made me a little uneasy, but I didn't know why. I also had one dream which was very distinct; in it I was bathing in an alabaster pool of clear water which had lilies floating in great abundance. As I washed, the words came clearly into my head, *"As you are washed in this water, you are cleansed of all your sin."* I remember feeling great joy, and I began to awaken. As I came into the waking state, I heard a very grating yell, "No, no, no!" and when I was totally awake I found that I was terribly distressed by the dream. I could not understand the significance of it all because I had been taught that the only way to be cleansed from sin was through indemnity. As a Christian, I am amazed by the significance of it, but in retrospect I can remember many similar incidents through which it is plain that God, my Father, was trying to get my attention and show me the terrible fallacy of my beliefs.

In February of 1974, I received a phone call from Mary. She was very excited by the fact that Moon was going to speak in Laramie! She offered to pay for my plane ticket if I could come to Laramie and help with the preparations, and then stay for the speech. Of course I too was extremely excited about this good news. My mother agreed to care for the children while I went.

When I arrived in Laramie, the whole "family," as we called ourselves, was in a great uproar. Everyone had moved out of the center—a big, old two-story house across the street from the campus of the University of Wyoming—and had moved into a motel. I was assigned to the preparation of the house, and it was amazing to me that so many things could be done to one house! I was overjoyed to see everyone again, although many of the members who had been there in the beginning had by that time been sent back east for various reasons.

Seeing Mary was, of course, the paramount thing, but there were other members with whom I came to develop very close ties. For example, there was one young girl named Donna who was as dear and sweet as she could be, and who later was totally broken by the severity of life in the Unification Church. In addition, there was a young girl whose name was Abby, and who was just a new member, and with whom I worked very closely on the house.

It was interesting that we had more young men than women in Wyoming from the very first, and there was one young man named Greg who was truly like a brother to me at that time. He had lived in the center at the same time I had, and had been a wonderful help to me with the children. He had a bright, sunny, vigorous personality at that time, but he was to change in a very disturbing way in the years to come. Another young man who was a very dear brother was named John. He was an exceptionally gentle, kind, and understanding person, who was also very good with the children.

I emphasize again that the people I met in Wyoming were very special, and did not possess many of the personal characteristics which I found in members in other parts of the country. I know that when these people were sent to other geographical areas of the Unification Church, they usually either changed dramatically or broke emotionally. It just tears my heart apart to think of the fate of these loving, gentle people. There was another young man, very young and refreshingly tenderhearted, named Lance. I have no idea what ever happened to him.

There were other members in the group then, but these were the ones to whom I was the closest, and about whom I heard later.

We all worked incredibly hard, and were very close to one another. We nearly tore the house apart and put it back together again, including making new curtains, painting, cleaning every corner, nook and cranny in the whole house, and, with the passing of each day, we became more and more frenetic. By the time the bus team arrived, we had worked ourselves up to an absolute frenzy of activity.

I had been told that since I was the first "sister" in Wyoming, I could stay in the house while Moon was there, and help serve him. But because I had come down with a bad cold, it was decided that it would be safer for Moon and his retinue if I did not stay in the house. However, I was asked to serve Moon, his wife and her caretaker, Mrs. Kim, Mr. Salonen, the president of the American church, and the Moons' interpreter, Colonel Pak, at the auditorium before the speech. I was absolutely delighted. I was given the money to go to the store and buy the things for them to eat, and was also told that none of them would eat dinner until the talk was over, so they needed a snack to eat beforehand to tide them over. I remember going all over town to find the things they wanted. Only Moon, his wife and Mrs. Kim ate; the others just had something to drink. I bought juice, cookies, fruit, and some other things, then went to a health food store to find raw cashew nuts. I could barely contain my excitement because by that time there was no doubt in my mind whatsoever that Moon was indeed the Lord of the Second Advent. Indeed to be privileged to buy the food that he would eat was more than my mind could handle.

I was also instructed to prepare the various dressing rooms for them to use before the speech, and I felt that this was an outstanding honor for me to be able to do this in service to Moon and his wife. We had secured the auditorium in the new Fine Arts Building for the speech, so I had to find rooms in the same building which would serve as dressing rooms. There were already two small dressing rooms below the stage level, but these were to be used by Colonel Pak and Mr. Salonen. So, my job was to acquire an adequate room for Mrs. Moon and Mrs. Kim to use before the speech, and a room for Moon to use. As a start, I was able to secure use of one of the music rooms and fix it up with furniture and room decorations from the set room of the drama department for Mrs. Moon and Mrs. Kim.

It was a little more difficult to find the right room for Moon to use. First of all, it had to be a room which could be completely blacked out. This seemed strange to me, but I was told that Moon always spends time alone in a completely dark room praying just before each speech. It seemed strange at the time that the room had to be completely black for him to be able to pray the way he wanted to pray. Secondly, the room had to have an easy chair, and be completely cleaned in every crack and corner. I was finally able to locate a small room with no outside windows and only one small window in the door which could be blacked over. I then secured an easy chair, a small table and a lamp.

Everyone else had taken care of the arrangements for the banquet and the speech. The stage was set, and we were worked to a pitch of excitement. In fact, we were brought to an emotional state with which I was later to become well acquainted, that of being physically exhausted, but so emotionally worked up that we were really in a hyperactive condition.

The plane carrying Moon and his entourage was to land in Laramie in mid-afternoon, but by noon there was quite a blizzard raging, and the plane was not able to land in Laramie. Therefore, Mary and several of the highest members of the bus team drove to Cheyenne to pick everyone up there. It is interesting to note that I had a rather troubling thought at the time. I knew that Jesus had been able to calm the storm of the sea by just commanding the winds to cease. Why couldn't Moon do the same thing? I had been told that because this was a new dispensation that Moon didn't work miracles, but nevertheless I was troubled—just for a moment.

We had all gone back to the motel to prepare for the banquet that evening. I loved being with the girls in the "family," especially at that time because there were many European and oriental members of the bus team. It was a beautiful thing for me to have such a close link with people from all over the world. I knew this was the kind of unity God desired for His people. It was not until much later that I found out that Satan does a very good job of counterfeiting God's will, and this I was only able to discern when I had seen true brotherhood and love as given by the Holy Spirit because of Jesus Christ.

The banquet was held at the country club, but the turnout was not very large because of the blizzard. All of the members of the "family" were there in full force, pouring out all the charm we could muster to impress the townspeople. Moon was also concentrating on charming everyone he met. I don't remember being particularly impressed by what he said, but I had myself so psyched up just to see him that I think he could have said almost anything and I would not have known the difference. We fell into bed exhausted that night, for our allotted few hours of sleep.

The next morning, we were to have a private meeting with Moon. I was unusually excited as we entered the house the next day. We all filed into the room where Moon was, bowing deeply to him, as we entered. He stared piercingly at each one of us as we entered. I remember that he spoke insistently of our need to give everything for what had to be accomplished, and at one point he singled me out and asked how long

I had been a member. By then I had been in for a year, but at that moment I had no doubt whatsoever that I would be a member for the rest of my life.

That evening we arrived at the auditorium very early to make sure everything was perfect. When it was time for Moon and his retinue to arrive, we made a pathway of members from the front door to the elevator. As he entered with his bodyguards, he looked neither to the right nor to the left and had a look of great disdain to his face. He soon neared the elevator where I was stationed, and I became aware of two students standing behind me, who did work-study as janitors in the building. They watched as Moon neared the elevator, then one whispered to the other, "I can't imagine why they worship him the way they do. He acts as if they are dirt beneath his feet!" Temporarily, I was greatly disturbed by his comment, but I did not allow it to dampen my mood for more than a few moments. Moon then went straight to his dressing room, at which time I served him his tray of fruit, nuts and juice and also took a tray to Mrs. Moon and Mrs. Kim. I left coffee for Colonel Pak and a package of No-Dōz for Mr. Salonen.

I then went back to wait outside Moon's dressing room, and as I climbed the stairs, I saw that everyone outside Moon's door was in a flurry, running around and yelling. I was alarmed and ran up the rest of the stairs. When they saw me they called, "A mirror, a mirror! Where is there a mirror?"

"A mirror?" I thought, "Why do they need a mirror?"

"Father [that's what we called Moon] wants a mirror!" one of the other girls said. "He's really upset because there isn't a mirror!" Well, I searched frantically for a mirror, but could not find one anywhere. As I returned defeated, Moon rushed out of his room and toward the stage. One of the girls from the group that traveled with Moon on the speaking tour was just standing there shaking her head. "A mirror! He's never wanted a mirror before. Oh, well." She shrugged and wandered off toward the auditorium.

Moon's speech was the same one I had heard in Denver. There were many young Christians in the audience with their Bibles, and as he spoke I noticed that they were flipping through their Bibles and shaking their heads in disagreement. As the speech progressed, more and more of them got up and left. It made me angry that they could just walk out on the Lord of the Second Advent like that! Boy, would they be sorry when they found out who he really was! And I knew they would certainly have to pay much indemnity for their actions. By the end of the speech there were, for the most part, family members left in the audience. I know now that Moon had struck out with those young fundamentalist Christians because they knew their Scriptures well enough to recognize heresy when they heard it! I later found that this was universally the case, and that it was a waste of time to try to even talk to them. The "Principle" rationalization for this was that the Christians would reject Moon the same way the Jews rejected Jesus.

I had to leave Laramie early the next morning to complete the final details pertaining to the divorce and to make preparations to move back into a center. Coincidentally, the only flight out of Laramie was the same flight Moon and his group were taking. I therefore went to the airport with Mary. Before they all boarded the plane, Colonel Pak and a woman named Dr. Lady Kim shook hands with all the members there. Dr. Lady Kim was reputed to be completely open to the spirit world, seeing all the spiritual activity around her. As she shook everyone's hand, she hurried along with her head bent, not looking anyone in the face. When she grasped my hand, she gave me a startled glance and appeared to look over my right shoulder. She jerked back her hand and turned quickly to go. I was terribly disturbed. What had she seen? For a change, I noticed that I sensed no evil with me.

Now, I fully believe that Lord had His hand on me even in the midst of hell, for He says, "No one can deliver from my hand, I act and no one can reverse it" (Isa. 43:13, Jerusalem). I believe that because of my free will, I was enmeshed in a trap of deceit, but our God is a faithful God, and He knew the desire of my heart to do only what He wanted me to do. I believe Dr. Lady Kim somehow sensed that I belonged, in the end, not to Satan or Moon, but to God the Father through the death and resurrection of Jesus Christ. There were many other startling incidents where I know the hand of God was moving in amazing ways during this period of darkness.

## 5

# *The Trap Snapped Shut*

It had been decided that I should be sent to Berkeley, California, where there was a center with other mothers and children. I was extremely excited because I envisioned reexperiencing the sharing of responsibility for the children and working for the church that I had experienced in Wyoming. I also had a love of the Bay Area from having previously lived in Palo Alto, which is south on the peninsula from San Francisco. As the time quickly approached for me to leave, the tension and excitement mounted. My parents were not pleased at the prospect of my taking the children and going to California, but at that time it was not possible to reason with me. My folks have since told me that I was exceedingly difficult to live with during the period when I stayed with them. I was irritable, bad-tempered and thought and spoke almost exclusively of the Unification Church, Moon and the "Principle." They said I could not even carry on a rational conversation about my commitment. In retrospect, I do remember feeling a tremendous spiritual arrogance toward them and everyone else who was not a member of the cult.

One night shortly before my departure, I entered the room where the children were sleeping. Suddenly I felt tremendous fear for their well-being. I began to cry and say, "O Father, what is going to happen to these children? They don't even have a father anymore, and I don't know what lies ahead for them!" At once, I heard a voice as clear as could be. It was a voice tremendously strong, yet incredibly gentle, and it said, *"You of little faith, your children have a father. I am their father. No matter what happens, you must trust in me."* I was so taken aback that I just sat motionless for a moment. Then I melted into sobs, touched by that indescribable gentleness and tender love I had not experienced for so long. I could not understand then the implications of what He had said to me, but I knew I must cherish it and keep it close to my heart.

When the day finally came for our departure, my mother cried. At that time she did not realize what we had become involved in, yet she sensed from what I had told her that it definitely was not of God.

We flew first to Laramie to spend a few days with the "Wyoming family." During this time, Mary told me some things which disturbed me. For example, she warned me that I must be prepared for what I might find in the Bay Area. She then launched into a history of the Unification Church in that area. It was, I found, a far-from-idyllic situation, because there had been much rivalry, bitterness and tension among members in the area. She told me that in the beginning, Miss Young Oon Kim, the woman who had translated the red "Principle" book into English, had been sent as a missionary to America, where she initiated a center in Berkeley. Sometime later a man named Mr. Che established a center in San Francisco. Mr. Che did not openly proclaim his organization as being the Unification Church, but rather, he devised a preliminary lecture series which talked broadly of general values and idealism; it was not primarily a religious lecture. His approach was highly successful as far as bringing new members in was concerned, and he even had to purchase several buildings to house his members after a while.

At the time I was to go to Berkeley, there was a Unification Church center there, which openly declared its affiliation with the national Unification Church, and there was also Mr. Che's group in San Francisco which followed his methods, and did not publicly claim to be part of the Unification Church. I was told that in years past, there had been much feuding between the two groups, but that now there was an attempt at reconciliation. At the time I thought it very strange that some of the San Francisco members didn't even know about Moon for literally months after their indoctrination.

Mary then proceeded to tell me more. There was, lo and behold, a third group in the Bay Area known as the "Oakland family." This group turned out to be a mystery to me for several months. All I knew at that point was that the group was headed by a Korean woman, and that her group had nothing at all to do with the other Unification Church group in the East Bay. They referred to themselves as the New Education Development, I believe, but were soon to be called the Creative Community Project. This group publicly denied any connection with Moon's Unification Church, and it was interesting to me that they were bringing in more new members than probably any other group in the country at that time. I was told that they would never have anything to do with other Unification Church members even if they were to meet us on the streets, and that I had just better stay away from them. As with the San Francisco group, their members did not learn about Moon for several months after joining.

All of this information confused and troubled me greatly. How could such bitterness and intrigue exist in the church of the new messiah? Why did these groups hide their belief in and loyalty to Sun Myung Moon? I finally decided to forget it temporarily and to wait and see what would happen.

The trip from Wyoming to San Francisco was miserable. Both of the children were airsick. Although I was so excited that I could hardly maintain my composure, at the same time I sensed darkness all around me. We arrived in San Francisco on a bright, clear afternoon. There was a woman there to meet us who was, in fact, the woman whose house was being used to house the children and some of the mothers. Her son was a member of the Unification Church, and she had recently joined herself. Her greeting to me was very formal and reserved, and I was somewhat disappointed. I had had such a close relationship with the Wyoming family that I simply expected to find that same kind of closeness in my new home. As I have said before, I never again experienced that kind of close, caring relationship anywhere else in my years in the cult.

We crossed the bay bridge and proceeded up into the Berkeley Hills. The drive was beautiful, and I was glad to be back in the Bay Area. As I was remembering my experiences in San Francisco, I still did not feel that sense of miracle, and I wondered at that. I was, however, full of expectation. The house was very nice, perched in the hills above the bay, and as we entered it, Sherry, the woman who had met us, explained that the mothers were all out working and that there was a girl who lived there and helped with the babysitting at home.

We entered a TV room which opened onto the kitchen and dining room, and I stopped short, appalled. There were half a dozen small children running wild, dirty and disheveled. The rooms reeked of urine, and several of the children were yelling or crying. Fear gripped my heart. How could they allow the children to be in this miserable condition? I caught my breath and quickly subjugated my thoughts and feelings. I knew from my extended study of the doctrine that all negative thoughts and feelings were from Satan. Then I caught sight of one lone adult slumped dejectedly in a chair. She was perhaps about my age, with dark hair and distinctive features. This person was one of the people whom I came to love dearly, and who ended up being destroyed by the coldness and utter disdain for humanity and compassion found in the cult.

As we came into the room, she jumped up and introduced herself as Sarah. I then met each of the children. They were all very individualistic, and some of them, I could tell immediately, were seriously emotionally disturbed. I vowed to myself to do all I could to help them.

As the afternoon progressed, I met some of the other members of the Unification Church in Berkeley. A couple of the mothers came home after a day of fund raising. I liked them all, but I soon came to learn that some of the mothers were on national fund-raising teams, or were about to leave to do that. There were a couple of the children who had not seen their mothers for months; these were some of the most severely disturbed children. This fact I found to be very threatening, but again, I subjugated my fear in the greater fear that I would give in to it and cause all three of us to be lost forever. I had been taught that if I were to leave, not only would I be lost to Satan, but all of my ancestors and descendants would have to pay for my faithlessness. I really believed that to take the children and leave would cost them their spiritual lives, and I had a terrible dread of my own spirit death if I left. We were taught that the spirit could grow only if the person was acting out the will of God, and that if one refused to do His will, his spirit would die, and Satan would claim him. I knew for certain that Satan existed, as testified to by the nights of terror when I had actually seen dark shapes in the room with me, and heard their terrible babbling! I was to have many more of these experiences before I was to be set free.

From the time I arrived in California, time had a funny way of escaping from me. I was occupied continually from the minute I awoke until I fell exhausted in bed at night. My days were a whirlwind of caring for the children and working for the Unification center. And big things were happening at the center! Within weeks of the time when I arrived, the center, which had numbered well over fifty members when I first came, had dwindled to a handful. Nearly everyone was either being sent back east for training or being sent out on national fund-raising teams. I soon found that the same thing was happening in San Francisco, although their center was clearing out at a slower rate.

The center directors at Berkeley were a couple who had been blessed in marriage by Moon several years before. They were very interesting people, quite opposite in their natures. The man was a gentle-spirited and deep-hearted person who had great love for mankind but who was in a constant state of what appeared to be confusion. He seemed to be under constant fire from his Japanese wife, who was as cold as ice. I always wondered if she had always been that way or if it was a defense mechanism.

The center, I was to learn, was in deep financial trouble. It was not long before I was called on to go out on a local fund-raising team for several weeks at a time. It was absolutely necessary for us all to pitch in to get the center back on its feet. All of the fund raising I had done in Wyoming had been fairly localized, and I had not been called upon to leave the children at all for any extended period of time. I was about to learn, though, that in the Unification Church, there is no respect for motherhood at all. For example, it was a general policy to separate mothers from their children as soon as possible. The children brought into the cult from outside were considered to be claimed by Satan, and therefore had no value to the group at all. They were disdained and literally despised by the great majority of the leaders I met. These children were therefore cast aside, and the mothers were encouraged to get rid of them as soon as possible. If the mothers could not do this, they were tolerated, but horribly mistreated. This entire nightmare was about to unfold before me, but at the time I was told to go out on the fund-raising teams, I had just an inkling of the overall situation.

Being on a fund-raising team in the Unification Church is a grueling experience. It is an excellent way to pay off much indemnity rapidly; this payment of indemnity was a major part of life in the cult. We were taught that we must pay in suffering for our own sins and for the sins of our ancestors, our nations, and the world. This suffering was done in installments of three-year periods. The first three years were dedicated to paying off our personal sins. In addition, the payment of indemnity was required to help fulfill certain conditions, such as achieving a fund-raising goal or bringing in a new person. It was, in fact, a matter of paying off Satan to come closer to God or to achieve certain things for God. What an impotent God we believed in! We were taught that God is totally dependent on how man carries out His will in order for Him to claim any victory on earth. I understood completely that my going out on fund-raising teams was a matter of paying indemnity as well as helping to accomplish the financial goals.

The instances that summer when I went out with a team were certainly fraught with the paying of suffering! We were usually in the towns in the San Joaquin Valley area, and it was incredibly hot every day we worked. It was August, so that it was not unusual for the temperatures to soar above 100 degrees. I was wearing gum-soled shoes, and by the time I had been out for a couple of days, they had melted flat; I resembled a duck flapping around the parking lots!

The worst of the suffering was not physical, however, although we often worked for fourteen to eighteen hours a day. The worst part for me was spiritual and emotional, and I often saw beings that I knew were not living people, and often they were fraught with darkness and had a feeling of terror about them. I also had much trouble emotionally with what we were expected to do. Spiritually, I had always been quiet and introverted, and now I was expected to be brash and aggressive. In other words, I was told that I should get that money any way I could. We were told that it might help if we didn't mention Unification Church or Sun Myung Moon unless we were directly questioned. It was, I was told, very effective to say I was from an interdenominational youth group, and that we were trying to help troubled youth to find a useful and productive life. I knew some members who clearly lied about what they were doing. We were made to understand that it was for the people's own good that they should give us their money. By doing so, they were unwittingly contributing to the building of the kingdom of heaven on earth. Not only that, but by giving up their money they were also paying a little indemnity. So it was for their own good, no matter how the acquisition of that money was accomplished.

There has been much talk about "heavenly deception" in the media recently. This was the rationale behind the practice of misrepresenting ourselves to the public in order to obtain their money. I had a very difficult time with the morality of the overall concept. But I knew better than to question my "center man," the person in charge of my group. It must be my problem, I thought, that it bothered me not to tell the truth about what I was doing and why. I also had a lot of personal pain and guilt about having left the children, but I was convinced that that burden was from Satan. We had been told that if we gave everything—100%—to what we were doing, God would protect the children. I was also to learn, before long, that this was not the way it worked!

I usually did fine—not outstandingly, but adequately—in my fund raising. However, I did have good days and bad days. If you were to have a bad day, it was encouraged for you to decide upon some way to pay some indemnity. Some of the more common methods for this were to stand under a cold shower for an extended period of time, or to fast, consuming only water, usually for a one-to-three day period. There were instances when we fasted for longer periods, but I was never encouraged to do a longer one while fund raising. It also helped, I was taught, to call forth your ancestors to help you influence the people. Calling upon your righteous ancestors for help was a rather common practice, although this type of invocation is expressly forbidden by the Bible. But then, I didn't know about that.

The summer passed quickly in a maze of fund raising and taking care of the children. There were some days when I actually enjoyed being alive again; these were the days spent with the children. We would often take them out to a local park for the afternoon, merely to get them out of the house, and these were sunshine-filled times when I very much enjoyed being with the children. I had always loved children in a special way, and I had been told many times by the teachers with whom I had worked, that I had been given a gift for relating to children. So, it was a special joy to be with these children, and also to have some time with my own children. I was just so thankful that my children were normal, well-adjusted children at that time, so very unlike the other children who were so very disturbed and hurting so very desperately. Yet, throughout the whole summer I had a constant feeling of impending doom.

# 6

# *But What About the Children?*

My feelings of doom and destruction were soon fulfilled. I was about to go beyond the face value of my experience in the cult and come to know the reality of what was being done to people. And I was about to taste the very fruits of the evil in which I was enmeshed. By this time, I no longer had any free will about what I did or thought. I will explain later the process by which people are brought to this state, for I was to become involved with the very heart of it within the next year. But for the present time, suffice it to say that I had no understanding of what was really going on. I knew only those things I was allowed to know: the surface, idealistic, public image that we were trying to project.

The first tinges of darkness began to creep in by the end of the summer. I began hearing, in private, from some of the older members, things which caused my head to spin, and my faith in what I was being taught to be heavily burdened. I remember being told that Jesus' real father was his uncle, Zechariah. I was told that Mary, under the guidance of God, was sent to sleep with her uncle that she might conceive Jesus, and that He would inherit all the payment of indemnity done by their lineage. I was shocked and hurt, but I was told to pray about it. I felt evil forces around me for days, and I knew Satan was after me. By then I had been programmed to believe that any time you hear truth, Satan would plague you. I also knew that I must subjugate all negative feelings and thoughts about the teachings because these were also from Satan. I finally decided to set it aside until I was able to accept it, because there were just some things, I had been taught, that we could not understand. But I also knew I must follow my "center person" and those who were older than me in the group. I was doing very well with the blind obedience required of us.

I had another disturbing experience shortly after that, while I was out distributing leaflets for a rummage sale that our center was having. As I walked down the street near the co-op in Berkeley, I had heard a girl scream. I whirled around and saw a young girl in tears, kneeling by her Labrador puppy which had just been hit by a car. She was crying, "Help me, help me! Oh, someone, please help me!" Everyone near her merely gave her a disgusted look and walked away. I could not believe people could be so callous. I ran over and asked what I could do, and she asked me to watch the puppy while she went into the store to get her boyfriend. When they returned and he saw the puppy, he began to sob. They had left their car at home and had no way to get the puppy to the veterinarian unless the boy ran home for the car. Again, he began begging for someone to please take them to a veterinarian, but no one would listen. I remembered seeing a veterinary office a few blocks away, but this was a Sunday, and I did not know if it would be open. The boy ran to get their car, and I ran to try to get help from the vet. I ran until I thought my lungs would burst, but unfortunately, no one was at the office. I returned just in time to see the young man arrive with the car, and so I helped them lift the injured puppy into it. I could hardly bear to see the young man and the girl crying, and the puppy bleeding so profusely. They thanked me enthusiastically and said I was the only one who had even stopped to see if I could help.

As they drove away, the immensity of what had happened to them hit me. Not one person on that crowded, bustling street had had enough decency to help those people when they were so obviously in pain. I could not understand how, even if a person hated dogs, anyone could turn away from the young people who were in such despair! I was physically sickened by the hardness of heart all around me and concluded that people cared only about themselves and had no compassion for others! I had seen it with my own eyes, and I felt like I had been physically beaten. How could we live in a world where people were so selfish and hardened? I grieved for mankind, because of the state of the world and the evil everywhere. I was glad I had found the new messiah (Moon) who could change people's hearts, for this was what we had been so heavily taught.

When I returned to the center, after stopping to compose myself after all the grief-stricken tears, I tried to tell the other members of the "family" what had happened. They all just stared at me with uncomprehending eyes. I should never have become involved with the whole thing, they felt. It had just been a waste of the church's time as far as they could see. I was shocked, to say the least. In fact, the implications of what had been said were so immense that I could not deal with the situation at that time. I simply felt numb.

I had been in the group for a year and a half by then, and I was beginning to be entrusted with attitudes and teachings that the world "just wasn't ready for." These new concepts are at the very heart and core of what is happening in the Unification Church. The heresies and the sick attitudes are carefully guarded from new members and the outside world. They are often revealed with a great air of confiding special secrets to members as those who are older in the group feel sure of the loyalty and maturity of that member. It was at this time that I was told that Moon really had had four wives and all but the present Mrs. Moon, whom we called "Mother," had failed somehow. It was not for us to try to understand what had happened, to try to fathom how the Lord of the Second Advent could have become involved in so many mistakes.

The end of the summer brought what turned out to be "the calm before the storm." The big Day of Hope speech at Madison Square Garden was scheduled for September. Everyone in the Unification Church in the Bay Area, except for the Oakland group, was to travel across the country, fund-raising all the way, to be in New York for the big event. A core group was left in Berkeley, and because of the children, we were the individuals chosen to remain. To tell the truth, I was quite relieved to have some time when I would at least know from day to day where I would be. It was a quiet time in which we maintained the schedule, but were at least able to minister to the needs of the children in some kind of consistent fashion.

Toward the end of that particular time, I had an experience that devastated me. That fall a new member had joined us, a girl who had actually joined in Boulder, Colorado, but who had come to the coast and moved into our house because she had a little boy a month older than my daughter (approximately one and one-half years old). We were taught that we must not be attached to our own children. We were also taught that these children came from satanic relationships and that although it was horrible to have "attachments" for any other person, it was most terrible to be "attached" to our own children.

The problem of attachment often was overcome by simply separating the mother from the child. For example, some of our children had not seen their mothers for over a year. We had another year-old baby who had not seen her mother for the great majority of her life. These were the children who were severely disturbed. But, if you were with your children, you constantly had to give evidence that you were not "attached." If your child was crying and another child was crying, you were expected to go to the other child. You were not allowed to minister to your own children at all if possible.

On one particular morning I came down for breakfast after having dressed one of the other babies. My own daughter, Julie Beth, was already sitting in a high chair. As I entered the room, she began to whimper and call "Mama, Mama." She held out her chubby, little fingers and beckoned to me. I put the other baby into his high chair and came around the table to give Julie a good-morning hug. Immediately the newer mother, Randi, verbally attacked me and accused me of spoiling my child. I did not know whether to scream or cry; how could you spoil a child who was in a situation of almost total emotional deprivation, a child who never knew from one day to the next whether she would even see her mother, a child who was, with no apparent consistency and depending upon who was caring for her at the moment, disciplined either not at all or with great severity? It was a totally insane accusation. I went into a rage against all the inhumanity I had seen in the months past, and had to leave the room. I never did forgive that girl for her cruelty and hardness of heart while I was in the cult. I praised the Lord that He has since shown me that she was operating from her own sense of desperation, and that He has given me the gifts of forgiveness and compassion for her now.

Shortly after everyone returned from New York, we received a desperate call from one of the mothers who had been on a mobile fund-raising team for approximately a year. She said she absolutely could not take it anymore, and that she was going to disappear if she wasn't able to leave the team. Chaos broke loose when we were told that the only way she could leave was if she was replaced immediately. In other words, one of us would have to go. Now there were five of us at the house: the middle-aged woman whose house we had lived in when I first went to California (we had since moved into a larger house owned by the group); my friend Sarah, to whom I had grown very close; Randi; myself; and another mother who recently arrived from another mobile fund-raising team. (She was the mother of the third one-year-old child and was having much trouble adapting to child care, and in fact, didn't really want to be near the children at all.) I knew that she, Randi, and I were the prime candidates (Sarah went through absolute mental torture while working fund-raising teams), but the pressure was heavily on me since all my experience had been with local teams. It frightened me very much to consider being on a national team, because I did not know if I would ever get back.

It had also become very apparent that I was the only

one of us who could tolerate being with the children for more than a couple of hours at a time; that is, the others could not cope with the disturbed behavior of some of the children, and it often drove them into a rage. I had great fear of what would become of the children because of their attitudes. As the pressure mounted, I had a growing sense of desperation; this feeling was accompanied by tremendous guilt for even considering the welfare of the children.

I knew I must seek the will of God in the most sincere way. In other words, I decided in desperation that I must pay some indemnity in order to seek God, so I set the condition for a three-day water fast in order to know what God wanted. During those three days, I was literally tortured by a horrible feeling of fear and threat. I knew that Satan was vigorously pursuing me, and I had to slip away continually so that the others would not see my tortured tears. I remember feeling as if I was an open wound walking around, and I could not imagine why I did not just die of the brokenness I felt. In essence, I thought I might literally die of a broken heart. I hated the thought that God did not seem to love those small, innocent children, and that He was allowing me to feel their pain of rejection so deeply.

On the night of the third day of my fast, I had three vivid dreams in succession. In the first, everyone in the center was getting ready to go out for the day, so I approached my center person and asked if I was to go. He said, "No, you are to stay here and care for the children." In the next one, everyone was packing to go out on a fund-raising team for the center. Again, I went to the director and asked if I was to go. Again he answered, "No, you have been chosen to care for the children." In the third dream, everyone was getting ready to board a big ship. I began packing my things when the center director came to me again. He said, "You are not to go. You *must* stay with the children." I awoke immediately and felt the tremendous presence of God. I had so rarely felt this presence since I joined the group that I was overwhelmed by it. I arose and prayed furiously that God would let His will be done. Later that morning, I told some of the others about the dreams, but they simply looked at me with disbelief. Nonetheless, I knew I had experienced God in a distinct way, and I waited to see what He would do. That afternoon, the leader of the mobile fund-raising team called the house. He said that if we were going to replace Marie, it had to be with someone who already had experience on a national fund-raising team, and who had a good record as a seller. The only one who vaguely fit that description was the mother of the other one-year-old girl. So she was chosen and was ecstatic about going. I grieved for the baby, but even when her mother was there, she seemed unable to nurture her baby in any way, and in fact, she seemed very resentful at having anything to do with her at all. That night I thanked God with all my heart for moving in such a direct way.

My reprieve was short-lived, however. One of the other mothers, who had a six-year-old girl, had been sent to Los Angeles to be on the California state fund-raising team. She was sent home shortly after Marie was sent back to our center. Not long afterward, a call came saying that she had to be replaced. I knew immediately that I would be the one who would be sent. I packed up my sleeping bag and my few belongings and put myself in the hands of God. I held my children, telling my oldest, Joshua, that I didn't know when I'd be back. They had told me it would just be for a few weeks, but I had a deep sense of foreboding.

Later, as I sat on the airplane bound for Los Angeles, the woman next to me tried to strike up a conversation. She was going to visit her grandchildren and wanted to know where I was headed. I knew there was no way that she, who was under the influence of Satan, could understand why I had to sacrifice my children for the salvation of the world. I turned my head so she would not see the tears coursing down my cheeks in response to the cruelty of it all.

# 7

# *The Death of Compassion*

I don't remember arriving in Los Angeles, because I was so numbed by pain. I believe that one of the brothers met me and took me to the center; I had heard about this center before, and this left me feeling somewhat threatened. Earlier that year a team of members from Germany had been assigned to Los Angeles because Moon had decided that we Americans were too "soft" and needed an example of sacrifice and dedication. Thus, he had brought teams from Japan and some of the European countries. The largest of the European teams was from Germany. We were made to understand that we could learn especially from the Germans and Japanese. I knew that although I would be on the state fund-raising team, which was comprised of Americans, we would be living in the center with the Germans.

The center itself turned out to be a converted motel. We arrived at night, and since it was late, I was shown to the rooms shared by the sisters. The German girls had the first room, while the American girls on the fund-raising team had the adjoining room. There was, of course, no furniture, but wall-to-wall sleeping bags. After I found an empty space and unrolled my bag, I fell exhausted into a deep sleep. The following morning began at about four-thirty. At that time I met the other girls on the team. Much to my relief, I found that most of them were originally from the old San Francisco family. They were warm and encouraging, and I even discovered that one of the other girls had a child living with her mother, so immediately I felt a kinship with her.

Our team had to arrive at the flower market in downtown Los Angeles sometime between 5:30 and 6:00 A.M. Our fund-raising efforts centered upon the making and selling of dried flower arrangements which were put into colored grain bases in decorative glass jars. These were called granariums, and we were able to make quite a lucrative profit on them.

I found that our team leader was a soft-spoken, good-humored young man, who was from somewhere in the South and who was a real joy to work for. The people on this team were very close to one another, and accepted me immediately. I was tremendously grateful for their warmth and understanding.

It turned out that I was to be the mother figure for the team, in that I would cook for them, do their laundry, and help make granariums. I was very relieved to know I was not expected to sell, because I detested the lying and fast-talking involved with selling. Our "factory" was located in the heart of Hollywood; in fact, we were just a couple of blocks off Sunset Strip. I settled quickly into my role, and my favorite part of the day was in the evening, when we all gathered after the dinner which I prepared in the factory for them, to make granariums. At that time we would share our days and uplift each other. The weekends were also enjoyable, because we spent more time together making granariums.

We spent very little time at the center. The Germans

and the few Americans there were organized into witnessing teams; they were having a pretty difficult time, which I could understand. It was not long before I became very much aware of the leader of the German team, who was the state director of California, and highly regarded by all. I was told that he had been an officer in the German Secret Service during World War II. He was like iron and had much charisma; the members worshiped him after Moon himself. Because he was the highest in the hierarchy in our area, he was the center person for all of us. I watched him and his German members in awe. I must say that I have never in my life seen people so cold, so completely devoid of human compassion and caring, as those people. They certainly did have the art of living for the cause perfected. As I continued to watch them, I was filled with a kind of horror. They were like automatons, having no apparent emotion except that of zeal and censure of the least infractions in attitude or deportment. To tell the truth, they frightened me, primarily because I could see no traces of human caring in them at all. I just thanked God that I did not have to work with them directly. I did feel sorry for some of their younger members who were still being broken, but I sensed that we were all bound for the same thing.

At this point, I realized that there were only two options: either to give in to the process of draining any kind of decent emotion from you, or to be destroyed by the cruelty demanded of you. The only way out, the only way to come to God, was to pay indemnity, and I was fast coming to understand that emotional suffering was much more devastating to the individual than any physical suffering. In order to live with and inflict and condone that kind of suffering, you had to let a part of you die.

I was a living mass of pain during that entire period. I felt great despair, but I suppose the factor which devastated me the most was the constant sharing of the pain and desperation that I knew the children were living. I prayed I might take on all of their pain so that they would be untouched by my absence. Further, I had to believe that God would honor my prayer. I had seen the devastation wrought in the lives of the other children by this kind of separation from their mothers, so I would rather die of a broken heart if it would allow my children to feel less pain.

The other mother and I would often awaken crying. We had to hide it from everyone at the center, but when we were in the van on the way to the flower market, the other sisters would allow us to cry, and hold us in the times of greatest despair. I knew it was sinful for us to cry and for them to comfort us, but the pain was so great that it sometimes overcame the guilt.

There were a few small comforts to our existence. When we did eat at the center, we were fed very well. It was at this time that I grew to adore granola mixed with yogurt for breakfast. It was the only time in my experience with the Moonies that my eating habits approached a balanced diet. The German leader felt that because his people worked so hard, they needed to be well fed to keep up the pace. His outlook on the matter was unique.

After I had been there for a while, my team leader came to me one day and asked if I would like to buy a small gift for each of my children. I could not believe my ears. I guess I just stared at him, because he had to repeat his offer. As I choked back the tears and thanked him, he said I could even call them. He seemed very disturbed at their ages; my little girl was only eighteen months old.

I proceeded to take action on his offer. The other mother told me that he usually gave her the same opportunity about once a month. I continued to find it difficult to believe his generosity, and I practically worshiped him from that time on, because I was so grateful for his compassion. It was desperately painful to hear those little voices, and to have to answer Joshua's, "When are you coming back?" with an "I don't know." I assured him that I loved him very much and that God would take care of him.

Not long after that, a brother who was just below the German leader in the hierarchy for California state came to check on our progress. He was of oriental lineage, and came from the old San Francisco family. He looked deeply troubled to me, as if the weight of the whole world was on his shoulders, and my heart went out to him. But, because I was so far beneath him in the organization, I dared not speak to him. In addition, I knew that we women were not supposed to talk to the brothers unless they spoke to us first. My team leader asked me to fix something to eat for this brother, Daniel, since he had not eaten that day. I had some oriental noodles with a broth that I could cook. As I was preparing this food, Daniel came in and showed me how to stir the broth when it boiled and how to stir an egg into the swirling waters. Again, I felt compassion and gratefulness for the gentleness I felt in his manner. Gentleness was simply not a characteristic which was nurtured in the cult. In fact it was one of the first to be eliminated.

Sometime soon after this meeting, my team leader came to me. "We're going to have to let you return to Berkeley," he said. I could not comprehend what he was saying.

Finally I stuttered, "But why?"

"Well," he said, "Daniel does not think they have any right to separate you from an eighteen-month-old baby!" My bags were packed and I found myself on the way back to Berkeley before I knew what had happened. It was not long after that I learned that both Daniel and my team leader had left the group, with Daniel leaving first. I was deeply grieved. How could God allow two such beautiful young men to be lost?

The situation was changing rapidly in Berkeley when I got back. The directors of our Unification Church center there were about to be shipped back east, and there was already a team of German witnessers on the scene. We at the center where the children were kept were commissioned to make granariums for a selling team, the proceeds of which were to be used to pay off the debts of our church in Berkeley. This team was made up of several brothers who were sent in specifically for that purpose. Because of my background in the making of granariums in Los Angeles, I learned where and how to buy the supplies in San Francisco and helped to teach the others how to make the granariums.

It was a grueling schedule. We took care of the children and made granariums all day. At night, when the children went to bed, all of us, the sisters and the brothers from the selling team, would produce granariums until early the next morning. We would not even bother to undress for bed; we would just work until we dropped from exhaustion and then we would lie down in the children's rooms and get an hour or two of sleep. But we usually slept in shifts after we had established a schedule.

It was during this time that a Day of Hope speech by Moon was scheduled for San Francisco. A One World Crusade team came into the city and prepared for the banquet and our master's speech there. We had very little to do with the preparations because of our other duties. The woman who had housed us when I first came to Berkeley was the only one who worked on the campaign, and she was in San Francisco every day making preparations. One evening I had to accompany her over there for a reason I don't now recall. I went to the offices used by the public relations group from the One World Crusade in their preparations for the speech and banquet. As I entered, I saw one of the young men from our Wyoming family. I was delighted, because we had all been so close out there, and I had greatly missed that caring and closeness since coming to California. He recognized me and came over to talk. I saw him two times and was sorely grieved, because this young man who had been so warm and caring and enthusiastic in his early days in Wyoming had become cold and very arrogant; he wasn't even the same person I had known before. It was as if everything caring and human about him had been drained completely. Again, I was seeing the process for myself, and I knew that in order to survive the organization, this would have to happen to me, yet I was enraged about it. I hated the icy, arrogant, humanless beings that people were being turned into. But, for me, there were no options. I thought that these negative responses were instituted by Satan, and I prayed for victory over them. I was long past the ability to do any reasoning about the situation.

My negativism was quickly overridden by the fact that Moon was coming soon. I adored him, and lived in constant excitement at the prospect of seeing him again. It was my third Day of Hope speech, yet I couldn't wait. I was completely mesmerized by the presence of "our true father." He had tremendously powerful charisma, and when he looked at you, you felt as if he could see every single thing you had ever done, thought or felt.

After the Day of Hope speech, things at the center settled into a normal routine. Several weeks later, a team of German fund raisers came north to work. They were to eat in our center, and so we had to cook for about thirty extra people in addition to our other responsibilities. On that team was one of the mothers who had a little girl in our center when I first arrived. She had since put her child up for adoption, and the child was gone. I do not to this day understand what motivated her to do it, but she went to her team leader and told him a tremendous lie about us. In the Unification Church there is a strict moral code which is enforced among the unmarried members. The sisters and brothers have practically nothing to do with one another. For instance, if a girl was in a room alone, and one of the men had to come in there for some reason, she would have to leave immediately. Great lengths are taken so as not even accidentally to touch each other. Now on this German team, the leader seemed to place more-than-normal emphasis on teaching about all the horrible, ghastly things that could happen if women allowed themselves to be a temptation to the men. It was peculiar, because this particular woman who had originally been from our center seemed to have an unusually close relationship with this same team leader.

One day she went to him and said that she thought there were "fallen" things going on between us and the members of the fund-raising team with whom we had been working. She said that we were in the habit of going into the children's rooms at night in our nightgowns while the brothers were sleeping in the same room. Now I can't say for certain what the others were doing, but I had been sleeping in my clothes for months. Not only that, but we rarely slept at the same time anyway, since we slept in shifts and then for only an hour or two.

I was completely devastated. The leader did not even ask us about it. The members of his team simply stopped speaking to us. When I discovered what the reason was, I was enraged with indignation. If there was one thing I had totally and completely embraced about the "Principle," it was the fact that sexual misconduct was the very root of all sin. I had been extremely fastidious in my relationships with the brothers, primarily because of the tragedy and devastation of my marriage. I had a deep, seething hatred of anything that even hinted at a sexual connotation.

One evening as I came down the stairway at the house where we were living, I paused on the landing. There was a high window at the top of the stairwell. I looked up, and my heart overflowed with prayer as I searched the night skies through the window. "Father, only you really know what has happened, and what caused this lie to be told. But you know the very depths of my heart, and you know that I have not done anything wrong. Father, I don't care what men may think about me if you know the truth. I put myself in your hands in this whole matter." I began to weep, and as I did so, I felt the all-encompassing presence of God. Before I knew what was happening, I felt as if I was being lifted right through the window and out beyond. As this happened, I had the experience of being held close in the arms of the Father, and of being comforted as a little child. His tenderness and gentleness were so overwhelming that I could hardly bear it. Suddenly, I felt myself pulled back into the presence of my body, and I had to grab the railing on the stair to keep from falling over. As I stood there in wonder, I knew for certain that I truly was in the hands of my God, no matter what these men might think.

The selling team was immediately withdrawn, and we were left again in a kind of vacuum. During this time I became more and more aware that things were really wrong. This was not the ideal to which I had given my life. I had been searching for the reality of God, and these people did not in any way whatsoever show forth the reality of the God I knew. Something had to change, for I was almost in total desperation.

And something finally did yield so that my life in the cult was changed in a very dramatic way. Out of total desperation, I contacted the girl who had first brought me into the cult. I told her how I felt, and of my disappointment in my whole experience with the "family" group since coming to California. She said, "I know that things have been terrible out there for the past year. Just have faith. I can't tell you what is going to happen yet, but things are going to get better. Just remember why you're here, and how important you are to God." As I hung up the phone, I was determined to be patient until I knew what was going to happen. It certainly was a tremendous opportunity to pay much indemnity.

## 8

# *The New Beginning?*

By December everything had come to the breaking point for me. The girl who had brought me into the cult, my "spiritual parent" according to the cult, called me and said that she could now tell me what was going to happen. She was very excited by the news she had learned at a leaders' conference with Moon. Specifically, the whole leadership structure in the Bay Area was going to change, and the entire area was to come under the leadership of the Oakland family.

I was stunned, and I have to admit, very wary of this change. The woman who led the Oakland group was a real enigma to the rest of the Unification Church members. She was a Korean who had joined the group in Japan, and who had been part of the old San Francisco group after she had come to America. For some reason, she had been exiled to the other side of the bay, and had recruited a young woman with a degree in psychology. The two of them had built the Oakland group. This other young woman, Christine, had recruited two of her sisters and her brother from their home in Michigan. They had in turn brought in some of their friends, who recruited some of their friends, and so on. These core people comprised the staff of the Oakland group.

It was also interesting that their whole group was completely cut off from the rest of the membership of the Unification Church, and they did not even claim Moon in public. This disturbed me greatly, because I realized Jesus' disciples claimed Him openly. And, in fact, hadn't they received and used all of their power and authority in His name?

In addition, this whole group was notorious for doing things in a different way from the rest of us. Furthermore, they kept themselves veiled in an air of mystery. So, I was not sure at all that this reorganization was an improvement! Yet, I was assured by Mary that there was much more love in their group than I had encountered anywhere else on the West Coast.

The change in power took place rather quietly. There were very few individuals left from the Unification Church in the Bay Area anyway. For example, we had a minimum crew at the San Francisco house and at our Berkeley house. I believe there were five of us at the house where the children lived. The first significant event that happened was that everyone who did not have a child in the center was sent back to Tarrytown, New York, for more training. At about the same time, we who lived with the children were invited to meet the Korean woman who was in charge of the Oakland group. We were all very nervous, to say the least, since we had all heard such strange things about her, including the rumor that her members almost worshiped her, nearly to the exclusion of Moon himself. I determined immediately that I would never do that. I knew who the messiah was, I thought, and no one was going to take his place in my loyalty. Because of this resolution, I went to that first meeting with a great deal of skepticism, despite Mary's encouragement.

We were to go to the house where this Korean woman, whom older members called Oma, lived with her recently acquired husband, who was a college professor who had met Oma and had become involved with the group. His name was Dr. Dirk, and the two of them reigned over the Oakland group from atop a hill in a large, luxurious house in the middle of Berkeley. As we walked up the hill, our conversation was full of conjecture, and even apprehension. When we reached the house, we were aghast, because it was much more luxurious than we had imagined. It was built in the California hacienda style with a large open courtyard in the center, and in the center of the courtyard was a large swimming pool.

With much trepidation we rang the bell and identified ourselves. The gate was unlocked, and we followed our escort into the house. The inside of the house did the outside justice, for it was richly furnished. I could instantly see that the Dirks lived very lavishly. As one of the young women escorted us into the sitting room, we were greeted by Oma herself. She was a very commanding person, with a definite air of authority. She asked us to be seated and offered us tea. She asked for some background information on each of us, and proceeded to inform us that she would keep some of us in her group, and some of us would be sent to other parts of the country. She said that she felt the mothers should be responsible for their own children, and that the children should not be left in the care of a group in which the mother was not present.

I was highly encouraged by the tone of the conversation. She added that she was calling all of the other mothers back to get their children, that these mothers would have to take their children with them, and that she would have to see what was to be done with us and our children.

Meanwhile, the first thing to be accomplished was that each of us was to attend a weekend workshop at their farm in Mendocino County just outside a little town called Boonville. We would have to attend in two shifts so there would be someone at our center to care for the children. It was determined that several of the others would make the visit on the following weekend.

As we walked back to our house, there were mixed reactions. Randi had been enchanted, but then she had only been in the group for a few months, and had little tradition to overcome regarding the overall philosophy of the Unification Church. The rest of us had been in the cult for at least two years, and were not nearly as trusting of this woman's motives. As it turned out, we did indeed have much to learn about Oma's cunning and her manipulative powers.

Within a week it was determined that I was to accompany one of the members of the Oakland group to San Francisco to show him where and how I purchased the supplies to make granariums. It was then decided that we were to make several dozen granariums for Oma's use at a party she was giving.

The trip to San Francisco was a significant eye-opener for me. We took care of the granarium business and proceeded to check on some orders which had been placed at a large fresh flower outlet by the group. It became apparent to me that the Oakland group sold dozens of fresh flowers every week as their means of fund raising. I was highly impressed by the volume of business they apparently did, and their adeptness in the business. I was to learn that they also operated a janitorial business, and were soon to open a delicatessen/restaurant. Neither of these businesses claimed any connection with the group as a whole.

I was rapidly realizing that this Oakland group was a highly organized, highly disciplined, highly successful little empire in its own right. The people in this group impressed me as being highly motivated, success-orientated individuals—the kinds of people who had done very well in school, and had probably been leaders in their peer groups in the "outside world." I liked most of them immediately; there was an energy in them that I had not encountered for quite a long time.

That first weekend some of us were packed and ready to go to Boonville. It was a highly informal weekend, we were told, simply an opportunity to meet some of the other "family" members. When the others returned, it was with an air of rejuvenation that I could hardly believe. I was still skeptical, but this unfamiliar group was gaining my appreciation all the time.

We spent the next week very busily making granariums day and night until we had the specified number completed. I imagine we were being evaluated also, and it seemed that Oma was satisfied with our performance.

The following weekend it was my turn to be sent to Boonville. I was highly excited, yet I must admit that I went with a strong sense of skepticism. We were carefully coached on the way to the big house on Hearst Street, which was their main center, and were told that we must carefully watch what we said, since most of the newer members did not even know about Moon. We were not to allude to the Unification Church at all, as most people did not know that any other activities were conducted outside our group. My indignation was aroused, but I knew enough to keep my doubts to myself.

My experience that weekend was one which was to be repeated dozens of times in the next year. It all began with a dinner at the big Hearst Street house. This house had at one time been a sorority house for students at the University of California. Because of this, the group had immediate access to the campus.

As we entered the house, someone immediately welcomed us and took us aside to visit. There were two staff members with guitars, and we soon gathered in a circle to sing. It occurred to me that I had very much missed the music we had in our Wyoming family. Many of us had been musical in that group, and we used our talents generously in our meetings and family gatherings. This group seemed to have a real appreciation of the value of music in binding people together.

Following the singing, we sat on the floor around low, round tables to eat our dinner. As it turned out, there were several longtime members of the group at each table. The conversation was very general, mostly drawing the other guests out, and describing how wonderful the weekend was going to be. After dinner, we loaded into several Dodge vans to begin the trek to Boonville. We were kept constantly busy during the trip singing and "sharing" with one another. I felt that the cult members seemed at a loss as to know how to relate to me. I had been in the organization longer than many of them, and since some of them did not even know about the Unification Church, I had to maintain a low personal profile. I had the definite impression that other than the staff members, there were not very many individuals who really had any idea of the scope of what was going on.

We arrived in Boonville late at night, and it was raining gently as we turned off the road onto a small dirt lane. We wound through what appeared to be a fruit orchard and across a level area that looked as if it were cultivated. We suddenly went down a hill and into a parking area. We unloaded our sleeping bags and followed the group members down a trail to the edge of a rushing river over which had been built a little foot bridge. The air smelled of rich, wet earth, and I fell in love with the land almost immediately.

We were guided to the first of two large trailers, and as we unrolled our sleeping bags and lay down to sleep, I thanked God the Father profusely for coming to my rescue in this way. I felt at home for the first time in many, many months.

Early the next morning we were awakened by the strumming of a guitar, and the enthusiastic chorus of "Red, Red Robin." I jumped out of my bag and was dressed before most of my companions were even out of their bags, because my reflexes were quite finely honed after two years in the cult. We were ushered outside to participate in physical exercises which varied in tone from Air Force training to yoga. After the calisthenics, we were divided into groups and introduced to our group leaders and their assistants.

This entire process, I was later to learn, was a finely geared machinery of indoctrination. It appeared that active cult members were in at least a two-to-one relationship to new people. I also noticed that the new people were carefully flanked at all times by a cult member, so that there was no opportunity for the new people to affect one another. We were given granola for breakfast with some orange juice, and I again noticed that most of the cult members did not eat. I realized that they must be fasting to pay indemnity to help the new people to join. During breakfast, all of the cult members shared how wonderful their lives were, and how very fulfilled they were by their lives in the group. Most of the new people's testimonies were quite paltry in comparison.

My group leader's name was Daniel [David], and he was a very winning, energetic young man. He had a good grasp of the dynamics of group action, I felt, and I could measure many of his techniques by the things I had learned in my course at the University of Wyoming. These people really knew what they were doing, I decided.

We had lectures all morning, with intermittent group discussions to reinforce the teaching. After lunch we engaged in a rowdy, and at times, even a violent game of dodge ball. Afterwards, there were more lectures and group discussions. During dinner, we were commissioned to create a song or skit within our individual groups to be presented to the overall group. These presentations were to be based on themes from our experiences and teachings that day. This encouraged a tremendous feeling of kinship with the other members of our groups. It was an enjoyable evening, and we subsequently fell into our sleeping bags completely exhausted.

The next morning was a repeat of the previous day, in that the lectures were basically innocuous. They were nothing like the ones I had originally heard. I could see shadows of the "Divine Principle's" teachings in them, but there was not really anything that anyone could take exception to. I noticed that there was much activity among the cult members during these lectures; they seemed to anticipate everything the lecturer was saying with great expectation and exclamations of affirmation. There was a fair amount of clapping for particular points brought home by the lecturer, and much nurturing of the new people during the whole presentation.

Toward evening the pressure and expectancy mounted noticeably. It was at dinner that each person tried to convince the new person he had been taking care of to commit himself to staying for a week. Some of the newcomers could not agree to it fast enough, but some of them had to be taken aside by the group leader before they assented. A large number of the new people agreed to stay, to the delight of the cult members, and those who did not agree to stay were contacted daily in most cases in an attempt to convince them to return for another weekend.

At the end of the day on Sunday, I actually found myself sad that I could not stay for the week, but there were many details which had to be attended to in Berkeley. The other mothers who had been summoned to return to get their children were arriving and departing at an erratic pace. Some had to come from as far away as the East Coast, and others from as nearby as Los Angeles. Several of the children had already been taken to uncertain situations in other parts of the country, and some were being deposited in other centers, in a manner similar to the way they had been deposited in our center.

The big question to be faced now was what was to be done with those of us left in Berkeley with our children. Not long after I returned from the weekend we were again called to a meeting, only this time it was to be at our house. We waited in great expectation to hear the verdict and were told that all of us would be moving to the land; that is, we would all live on the farm outside Boonville. In addition, we were told that we would be given a trailer in which to live, and that it would be so good for the children to live in the environment of the farm. We were delighted for the most part, although there were many details which seemed very hazy to me; but, I was ready to go.

The day was set for us to leave, and we began to pack. People kept telling us that we really didn't need all the things we were packing for the children and the trailer, but their point did not really register with us. As the designated day came near, we were all filled with mounting excitement.

# 9

# *Follow the False Hope*

The day of our move to the north dawned fresh and golden, and we were filled with excitement. The group included Marie and her five-year-old son, Jimmy; Randi and her one-year-old son, Dorien; myself and my son, Joshua, who was three, and my daugher, Julie, who was one; and a two-year-old girl named Jessie, whose mother, Betsy, was already on the farm.

To our great surprise, one large, dilapidated flatbed truck pulled into the driveway. A man, probably in his fifties, got out of the truck, and told us he was to move us to Boonville. We were stunned. How could we all possibly ride up in the cab of that truck? However, ours was not to ask how or why, but just to do what we were told, as with everything else in our lives. We loaded everything onto that old flatbed truck, and then we all squeezed into the cab. As we pulled out onto the highway, I remember thinking we surely did look like something out of *The Grapes of Wrath*, and I had to chuckle to myself despite the discomfort.

As we drove along, the man began to talk to us. His name was Nat and he was part Yucca Indian, he said. He had raised a number of foster children, and enjoyed children greatly. As he talked, I thought he was quite a character, and I could not imagine how he fit into the Unification Church. He said that he had first met the group in San Francisco—"in the old days" before everything had begun changing. He had enjoyed the people, and so he remained with them. He had been living on the land (the farm in Boonville) for a while and helped with the actual farming. He lived in the loft of the barn, and he commented to us that we would be living near him. The entire conversation was very interesting. At one point something fell from the back of the truck, and we had quite a laugh over Nat's attempts to retrieve it from the middle of the traffic. All in all the trip was quite an experience.

After we passed Santa Rosa, we took a less traveled, winding road into Boonville. As we approached the town, the children were brimming with excitement. On the south edge of Boonville I recognized the dirt lane which turned onto the property. I also saw the wooden sign, "Ideal City Ranch." We turned into the lane and wound through the orchard until we could see a fence and gate, beyond which there was a barn. Tucked next to the barn was a small camp trailer. "Well, here's your new home," Nat announced. We stared at each other in disbelief. How could four adults and five children live together in that tiny camp trailer?

"Oh, it must be a mistake," Randi implored.

"Nope, no mistake," Nat replied. "Better start getting unpacked. Though I don't know what you're going to do with most of it, cuz' it sure won't fit in there!" We unloaded the truck in a daze, wondering what in the world was going on.

We did not have to wait very long before we were all summoned to the trailers where the training sessions were held. There we were to meet Micah, the director of the facility in Boonville. He had a room in the first trailer, so that is where we went. He greeted us warmly, and said he was glad to have us as part of the family there. The whole matter of our problem with living space was adeptly ignored, and I certainly knew better than to bring it up. All in all, I liked Micah's attitude, and he was somehow able to assure us without ever mentioning the existence of any problems.

We were left to return to the small trailer by the barn, and as we walked up the road, I marveled at the beauty of the land again. I felt that just because I loved the land so much that things would have to take a turn for the better.

Within the next couple of days, Marie and Betsy were sent to New York, leaving their children in Boonville. Randi and I were left to care for the children.

In actuality, things were even worse than I had first suspected. In addition to the quarters being terribly cramped, we had no running water, no heat or electricity, no indoor bathroom facilities, only an old outhouse equipped with a bucket, and much to our dismay, the roof leaked. Well, it was the middle of the rainy season in Northern California, and within several days we awakened to the sound of rain beating down on the roof of the trailer. As the children awoke, they began to complain of being wet. We soon found a large leak right over the bed where the three older children were sleeping. About the time we got the blankets yanked off the bed, there was a loud knock at the door, and as I opened it, I was greeted by the shining, smiling face of one of the "brothers." "Well," I said, "if it isn't a bit of sunshine." The children giggled as the young man entered, because he was totally engulfed by a large, bright yellow raincoat. He hesitantly stepped inside and said that he was on the farm crew which took care of the farm chores, and that he wondered if there was anything we needed. We told him that his timing was just perfect, and that, indeed, we did need some help. We showed him the leak, and he immediately went to find the materials to fix it.

I was greatly encouraged by this visit, because this was the first person I had met in the cult since my time in Wyoming who seemed to have any compassion or caring at all. His very presence was a calming influence in the turbulent months ahead, as he seemed to be one of the very few people on the farm who had any compassion for the children at all.

Our first few weeks in Boonville were very hectic. For the most part, we had to keep those five, energetic children confined to the trailer at all times because of the rain. However, on the few days when the sun fought its way through the clouds, the children ran and played like little puppies, delighted with the space and freedom afforded by living on a real farm.

On these sunny days we took them on walks to explore our new home. We found that several acres just to the east of us were under cultivation, and that the brothers on the farm crew really did do the chores of a farmhand. Further east on the road, toward the hill which dipped into the parking lot for the training sessions, was a chicken coop and a fenced area which housed a huge red sow named Clarabelle. This discovery delighted the children, and we were frequent visitors to the animals.

We were made to understand that the area beyond the hill toward the parking lot was off limits to the children. Because there was always a training session in progress, we had to hide the children from the new "trainees." It was the consensus of the staff that these new people would not understand. What they would not understand was never verbalized, but I had the suspicion that it was the fact that most of these children were not with their mothers, and some of them had not been for a very long time. I consciously suppressed this thought though, because it followed that if this fact had to be hidden from the public and the new members, then there must be something wrong with the situation. And I knew that any negative thoughts about the group and their practices were from Satan and had to be overcome.

It was not many weeks before Randi was commanded to come down to the main training facilities to take part in the training sessions. Not long after she was ordered to do this, it became very apparent that she was gone permanently. They made it impossible for her to visit her child, and both she and her little boy suffered a great deal over the situation. During this time, I tried to give extra amounts of cuddling and nurturing to the child, whose name was Dorien. Yet as I watched, his sunny enthusiastic disposition began to deteriorate. He began to grieve for his mother, and nothing I could do seemed to be enough. He became quiet and somber, and the change in him broke my heart. He was not even two years old yet, and he was having to bear pain that most adults never have to face. His young life, as far as he could tell, was full of rejection from his mother, which closely followed the rejection he had experienced when his father disappeared from his life at the time when Dorien and Randi moved into the cult, a few months before. I was to see this syndrome of rejection, followed by self-rejection and self-hate and grieving, in at least ten children while I was in the cult. Some of these children developed terribly disturbing patterns of behavior.

For the time, however, I was left with Dorien, Julie Beth, Jessie, whose mother was in New York, Joshua, and Jimmy, whose mother had also been sent to New York. At four and a half, Jimmy was the oldest; Josh was three and a half, Jessie was two, and Julie and Dorien were one and a half years old. Because it was still raining nearly every day, I tried to find things we could do in that cramped, little trailer. I searched for and found a small portable record player and got out the records we had brought from Berkeley. The young man who had patched our roof, whose name was Ira, visited us regularly, and had the foresight to run a very long extension cord from the barn to the trailer. Because of this cord, we were able to run the record player and plug in a lamp at night. I spent many hours playing Walt Disney records, and encouraging the children to act out the stories and to dance and sing with the records.

There were moments of laughter, but it was very difficult to draw most of the children out of the consuming melancholy which engulfed them.

Another major problem which had to be faced was the fact that there was no way to prepare food for the children. The stove had no source of power, nor was there any electricity to operate the refrigerator. This meant that every day I had to leave the children to walk down to the trailer where the kitchen for the training sessions was located. I had to wait until the trainees had eaten and were gone, and then I was allowed to sneak down to collect the leftovers for the children and myself. There were times when I literally had to beg for food for the children. It also worried me that there was very little nutrition in the food we were given. Consequently, the children were nearly always hungry.

As the weeks passed, I saw practically no one except the members of the farm crew. This group was led by a young man from New England whose name was Stan. He was several years younger than me and was perhaps the most driven person I have ever met. He drove himself and those around him mercilessly, and there were several times when he literally drove himself to exhaustion. I did not know exactly why he was that way, except that it appeared that he equated hard work with righteousness. From the very beginning, we were at odds. I could hardly bear to see his hardness of heart and apparent lack of any compassion, and I am certain he felt me to be unrighteous because I devoted so much of my time and energy to the nurturing of the children. It seemed that he had a great dislike for the children, which alienated me, yet now I am sure that he just did not know how to relate to them.

It also disturbed me that he seemed to have so little understanding of the "Divine Principle." The whole concept of Abel (whom the center person of any situation was to represent) serving Cain into submission, seemed to have never been absorbed by Stan. Because of that, I felt contempt and rebellion toward him. I know he did not care for me at all either. He felt, I am sure, that I should have been out working with the others on farm chores instead of frequently studying the "Principle" and copies of "Master Speaks" to keep myself fed spiritually. The situation was a very difficult one, and after a couple of weeks, we simply stopped speaking to each other. Yet I knew this was not right either.

As the weeks dragged on, I became more and more disheartened. The circumstances for bare survival were difficult enough, but they were compounded by the increasingly disturbed behavior of the children who had been separated from their mothers for a long period of time, and by the fact that I had very little contact with other adults. It was about this time that I realized my only help was in my Father in heaven. I therefore began praying that He would give His love for these children, because my love was not nearly sufficient. In His mercy, He granted me my request, and as I prayed every day, my love for these hurting, difficult children became something that I knew was not coming from me. It was really an amazing experience, and confirmed even more strongly my belief in a loving Father in heaven.

During this same period of time, however, Satan began more frenzied activity in my life. Late one night, I had gotten all of the children to bed and to sleep, and had read some "Master Speaks." It was approximately midnight when I turned off the lamp. At that moment, I had the urgent sensation that someone else was in the trailer. In absolute terror, I turned around toward the direction where I sensed the presence. As I stared into the near darkness, I saw a figure standing there as plainly as I was. This figure was somewhat like a silhouette, totally black. Yet I could tell that it was robed in a floor-length black cape and was wearing some sort of wide-brimmed hat. It was huge—touching the ceiling of the trailer with its hat. As soon as I saw it, my mind was filled with thoughts of violent rape and mutilation. I could not clear these terrifying thoughts from my mind, and in my panic and horror I sank to the floor gasping, "No, no, please no!" After a moment of shocked paralysis, I began grabbing wildly for my clothes, and as I began fumbling to put them back on, the creature began to laugh a grating, sadistic laugh. And I heard in my mind, "It's no use, nothing you do will make any difference." By this time, I was sobbing wildly. I grabbed the *Divine Principle* and began praying and singing "family" songs. Nothing helped. Finally, I crawled into the bottom of the sleeping bag, where I could no longer see the figure, except in my mind, and I finally fell asleep in total exhaustion. I slept in my clothes for months after that incident.

In the following months, it was not uncommon at all for me to see similar dark figures all around me. It did not seem to matter whether it was day or night, as I had as many encounters during the day as I did at night. One afternoon I was walking down the road alone toward the trailers where the kitchen was located. It was a bright, sunshine-bathed day, and as I neared the place where the road dipped into the parking lot, I heard much shouting and whooping. I thought at first that it must be a group of the brothers down by the river, but as I approached the river, I realized there was no reason for the brothers to be down there, or to be yelling like that. As I listened closely, it reminded me of movies I had seen in which a group of Indians were whooping and yelling. I became more and more puzzled, and began to run to a place where I could see the river plainly. When I got there, the voices stopped, and I was met with silence, and no evidence of anyone having been there at all. I was confused, but strongly suspected that the spirits were at work again.

It was strange that these spirits manifested themselves in so many ways. Some were not particularly threatening, such as this experience by the river; yet others were tremendously threatening.

Another night when I was alone in the trailer, I was again reading an article about cultic doctrine when the trailer began to sway from side to side. I was at first quite curious. It was a clear, calm night with no hint of wind at all. It occurred to me that it might be someone outside trying to play a trick on me, but I quickly discounted that idea because it was about two o'clock in the morning. I began to feel panicky as the trailer swayed more violently. At one point, I thought the trailer might go crashing over on its side, and in terror I drew aside the curtain to peer outside. My fears were confirmed as I saw that there was no one on either side of the trailer, nor were any of the leaves on the tree next to the trailer moving. I began to sob and sing those supposedly powerful songs and pray, but it had no effect at all. Just when I was sure that the trailer was going to tip over, the swaying stopped as suddenly as it had begun.

The next day Randi came up to the fields to work with the trainees. I was outside at the time, and she ran over to talk to me. She was very agitated and began to speak in hushed, hurried tones, proceeding to tell me that on the preceding night at about two o'clock she was walking to her sleeping bag. She said that as far as she knew she was the only one left awake, and so she was trying to be very quiet. She said that suddenly, the trailer began to sway back and forth. It first occurred to her that a strong wind must have come up, but as she looked out of the nearest window she could see no evidence of any wind at all. She began to feel a terrible fear as the trailer swayed more and more violently. After a few moments of confusion and fear, she decided that she had better awaken some of the staff. She said that as she stepped into the hallway leading to the rooms where the staff stayed, the swaying stopped just as suddenly as it had begun. She then lay awake for a long while, afraid to go to sleep.

I was amazed—and a bit frightened—to think these forces would even attack the trailer where the staff was staying. But I was relieved to know I hadn't imagined it all. I suppose that the aspect of the situation which disturbed me most was that no one seemed to have any effective power against these forces of darkness. I had found that I could use all the "holy salt" I wanted to, but it seemed to have very little power against these assaults. Moon himself was to have blessed the salt, which was used to bless more salt, and this was to be used as a tool of victory over Satan and his legions. Yet, in all my experience with evil spirits, not once did I ever see any decisive victory over the enemy. I was beginning to sense an oppressive presence of evil around me most of the time.

The situation on the physical level was rapidly deteriorating also. Another child moved in with us, the child of a long-term member of the Oakland group. He had been living in Berkeley with three older boys, two of whom were the children of Dr. Dirk. But because he was not yet school age, he had been moved to the farm. This little boy's name was Pepito, and he was a very serious, burdened little boy. He was just four years old, but the heaviness in his eyes made him seem older. He seemed quite distraught at being brought to the farm, and I soon discovered that he missed the boys he had been living with and the girl who had taken care of them. I assured him that all of them would join us when summer vacation arrived, which seemed to ease his mind. Before too long, however, I saw that this was not the real problem at all.

On Sunday evenings, when all the "family" members left to return to the Bay Area, one of the cars would stop in front of our trailer, and Pepito's mother would jump out. She would grab him up in her arms, and he would cling to her as if his very life depended on her embrace. She would carry on a short, light conversation with him, and then she would set him down and run gaily off to the car which awaited her. The minute she would set Pepito down, he would begin to wail. She would throw him kisses as he became more and more hysterical. By the time she reached the car, he would be screaming and crying and throwing himself on the ground. He would plead, and beg her to stay just a little longer, but his distress seemed to affect her in no way. That child would act as if his heart was breaking, and she would shrug it off as if he were not even a human being. This scenario was repeated week after week.

I began to notice a pattern in Pepito's behavior. It would take him until about Tuesday to get over the ordeal, and then he would become mellow for a couple of days, during which he allowed himself to become involved in the play of the other children, then sometime on Thursday afternoon, he would become more and more sullen. By Friday he would be incredibly tense, and all day Saturday, he would be an impossible discipline problem, having tantrums quite frequently. Sunday would be twice as bad as Saturday for him until the cars started winding their way up the hill toward the gate. This pattern was repeated like clockwork until I thought the child would explode with frustration, anger and grief.

I was not doing very well myself. The tension of trying to be all things to these desperate children was terribly taxing. The situation was compounded by the fact that I very rarely saw or spoke to any other adults. I was torn to pieces by my conflicting emotions and needs. I was desperate for some adult companionship that would take me away from the children for a while. These children were such a trial that I feared no one else would care enough to minister to their inner needs. It is horribly difficult to react in love to children who are hurting so badly that they go out of their way to retaliate with obnoxious behavior. I knew it was only with the grace of God that I was able to love them in spite of their behavior.

I fought with this conflict for several weeks, and then one Sunday evening while Pepito was enduring his ordeal of hysteria, I simply broke down. It was as if all the emotions I had pent up over the months of being alone burst forth, and I began to cry hysterically. I tried to hide my distress, but the final blow came when another car stopped and Daniel, the young man who had been my group leader on my first weekend training session on the land, stepped out. I have no idea why he stopped, but as he came nearer, I could not contain my tears. They began to roll down my cheeks, as I frantically tried to suppress them. Daniel could obviously tell that something was wrong, and as he began to question me, I lost control and began to sob. I blurted something about being so very lonely, and sobbing apologies at the same time. Daniel looked very concerned, and said he would do something about that. My heart dropped as I considered the implications of what he said, but fear, and struggle with the forces of evil, and the hopeless conditions surrounding the children had taken their toll. I knew that what I had said could not be taken back, and in my despair, I could not struggle with the worry of the implications of what might be coming. I feel now that I had fallen into a planned trap to separate me from my care and concern for the well-being of the children. Whether the plan was conceived by the forces of Satan, or whether it manifested itself in the minds of men, I don't know, but it certainly worked. I was to the point of feeling as if I was losing my sanity. Satan had me right where he wanted me, and my situation was about to change in what would end up to be a drastic way.

# 10

# *Respite*

Early Monday morning the effects of my outburst the evening before began to appear. A young girl appeared at the door of the trailer with orders for me to report to the trailers down the hill. Micah had gone somewhere, but one of the staff members from Berkeley was taking his place. To my great dismay I found that this was a young man named Stephen, whom I had never liked because of his terrible show of arrogance. My heart sank as I gathered myself together and hurried down the hill to the training area.

Stephen saw me as I came across the lawn from the river. He jumped up and greeted me warmly, asking me to sit down by him on the lawn. He proceeded to tell me that there was great concern for my well-being, and that it had been decided that I should have a day to gather my forces together. He suggested that I take a walk up in the hills and have a talk with God. He assured me that everyone wanted to help me in any way they could, and that I was to take the entire morning to reflect and pray.

With tremendous relief, I walked up into the hills to do as he had suggested. I found that I had changed my attitude toward Stephen entirely, and looked upon him with the fondness of a sister. In the months to come, the fondness grew as I discovered that he too had his moments of trouble and weakness.

I was totally thrown off guard by this show of care and concern. It has only been in the past two years that I have realized the extent to which this show of so-called love and caring was used as a tool to manipulate people into doing exactly what was wanted of them by the cult leaders. I fell right into their plan.

During that morning I did indeed pray. I was chagrined by my feelings of despair and helplessness during the weeks past, and I again totally dedicated myself to God's will, and promised I would "fight it out" for God. This was a common term used in the cult to denote that an individual had to endure suffering to pay off the indemnity required for salvation.

By the time I returned from my walk in the hills, I had an entirely new perspective. I had again become enchanted with God's creation in that place, and was filled with zeal for the mission of the group.

I returned to the little trailer by the barn with renewed vigor. The girl who had been sent to relieve me stayed the rest of the day to help me. It was a real luxury to have an adult with whom I could share. In fact, this girl became very close to me in the course of the next few months. Her name was Deborah, and she was only about nineteen years old. She had only been in the group for several months, but the blessing of her presence was that she had an enduring love for children, and she was very good with them.

In the weeks to follow, Deborah spent nearly every day with me. We enjoyed many pleasant hours together with the children. Often we would put Julie and Dorien, the smallest ones, into a wagon, and the others would trot along beside us, and we would walk into town to do our laundry and have a small lunch in the park. The children thought this was the greatest treat they had ever had, and we would always have a wonderful time.

During that same period of time, I began to be recruited to go out on selling and witnessing teams during the week. Deborah would remain behind to care for the children, and I would return the evening of the day I went out. I also began working with the teams sent into the fields to work. My favorite job in the fields was to work in the apple orchard, and I remember specifically one afternoon after we had been pruning the branches. We had worked hard and enjoyed being out in the sunshine, in the company of the work crew. As evening approached and it was time for the rest of the people to return to the training session, we strolled together down the road toward the trailers. The sky was beginning to be tinged with delicate shades of pink, and the smell of growing things in the warm earth was carried lightly in the breeze. I was filled with a sense of well-being and fellowship I had not felt since leaving Wyoming. A great love for God's creation and the people washed over me in a luxurious wave. It was one of those moments that etches itself on one's memory for all time.

At that time I also began being called to attend the weekend sessions. The intense energy of those sessions carried me from one week to another. Deborah was being assigned to be with me most of the time. We grew very close, and she was a tremendous help with the children. She had been trained well in the principle of serving her center person, who was me. In return, I, as the Abel person, loved her with encouragement and tenderness. Things were looking up greatly.

Early mornings were favorite times for me. The fog

would roll inland during the night, and would skim the ground in the early part of the day. Nat would often go outside and build a fire, over which he brewed what he called "cowboy coffee." We would sit near the fire in the dampness and watch the fog burn away in the growing sunlight. These were, again, moments of great contentment for me.

More improvements came with the arrival of spring break in the grade schools in Berkeley. The three older boys—Dr. Dirk's two and a third little boy about eight years old—were out of school for a week. The young woman who cared for the boys was the mother of the third boy; her name was Abigail. She and the boys traditionally spent the spring breaks and summers on the land, and this year was no exception. I found myself greatly anticipating their arrival, for I had met Abigail several times and liked her very much. To accommodate Abigail and the boys, another trailer was moved next to our small camp trailer. This was a much larger trailer, with three rooms, a bathroom and a storage area. It was an old trailer, with no carpeting or furnishings, but it seemed like a palace to me at the time. It was placed next to our trailer and set at right angles to us. I moved the children's belongings into the big trailer, and we all slept on the floor in it. This cleared the small trailer, and enabled me to leave the table set up to be used for meals.

Abigail and the boys arrived on a Friday evening, and there was a joyous reunion between them and Pepito. Abigail was appalled at our living conditions. She prevailed upon Stan to get the farm crew to dig a large hole under the outhouse to replace the bucket. She and Stan were great friends from summers past, and she did much to give me a new understanding and appreciation for Stan. She also had money to buy food for the boys. She asked me what the smaller children had been eating, and I gladly explained our situation to her. I was greatly concerned with the children's lack of nutrition because of an incident which had occurred a week before.

Julie Beth had been crying a lot and complaining about cramps in her legs and in various other places. It had gotten so bad that she could not sleep, and I had become quite worried about her. Because we had been expected by the cult leaders to get the children on the Aid for Dependent Children program in Mendocino County, we had medical coverage for the children and mothers on the program. We never saw a penny of the money because it was always signed over to Micah, but our medical expenses were fully covered.

It was usually discouraged by the leaders for anyone to go to the doctor because physical suffering was just more payment of indemnity, but because our medical expenses were paid by the state, we were able to get medical help for the children. Consequently, one of the members of the farm crew drove me to a hospital in Ukiah whenever one of the children would become sick.

I had taken Julie Beth to the outpatient clinic to find out why she had such terrible cramping and was so listless. The doctor did several laboratory tests on her, including some blood work. When the results came back, he conveyed to me that he was certain that she was very malnourished, and that I had better start ensuring that she would receive a more balanced diet or she would have much more serious problems than she already had. This verdict tore me apart, for I had always been extremely conscientious about the children's nutritional needs before I joined the cult. The only thing I could do was to pray with great intensity that God would somehow meet their needs.

When I told Abigail what had happened, she was totally outraged. She had been in the Oakland group for several years, and had worked in the household for the Dirks. She said she had always been given an allowance to buy food for the boys, and that she would speak to Dr. Dirk immediately about our situation. She did just that, and from that time on, whoever was caring for the children was given an allowance to buy food for them. The money was just enough to be certain that the children received a balanced diet, and I thanked God for hearing my prayers and moving so promptly to remedy our dilemma.

The week with Abigail was like heaven. I loved her so much, and we got along tremendously. She helped me to break the ice with Stan, and she also helped me to reach out in a new way to others. We had many deep conversations as we worked together. For example, I recounted to her some of the terrifying events of the past months, and was relieved to hear that she too often saw and heard evil spirits. She listened, amazed as I told her about the night I had been threatened by the tall, dark, caped figure with the broad-rimmed hat. She described it perfectly and told me that in past summers she had often seen that very figure standing on the side of the hills overlooking our trailers. She had first met it on one of these hillsides, and had much the same experience of terror and panic.

She proceeded to tell me that that was why we were not able to keep animals on the land. She said that in the early days, they had tried to keep a couple of dogs, but they just went crazy and finally ran away. I told her about the chickens we had had upon our arrival, and how they had refused to stay on our property, but had kept roosting at the neighbors until he had finally built a house for them. Even Clarabelle had run off, and been killed by a bus. I realized that even the animals had been aware of the evil which constantly surrounded us, and it gave me ominous feelings to learn that this evil even affected the animals.

Abigail also revealed to me that Stan was very open to hearing and seeing things of the spirit realm, and that this was why he seemed so haunted and driven much of the time. He had to keep going so as not to be constantly distracted by them. This gave me great compassion for Stan, and from that time on, I made an effort to be kind to him and not to alienate him.

I loved sharing with Abigail, and I enjoyed her optimistic energy. I was not ready for the week to end as soon as it did, but I looked forward with great anticipation to the coming of the summer vacation.

The weeks that followed were filled with activity and sunshine. The rainy season had spent itself, and the earth was bursting forth with new life. I spent much time working to get the young plants started and tended. I also went out on several fund-raising efforts in Ukiah and Santa Rosa. I still hated the deception involved, though it was more lying by omission than anything else. We spent many days in Santa Rosa, frequenting businesses and small industry, selling flowers and granariums under the name of the "Ideal City Ranch." We were encouraged to sneak into the businesses in the Industrial Park, and to sell as much as we could before we were caught and thrown out. I hated this procedure, because I had been carefully taught to be meticulously honest in my words and actions from childhood. I never did grow to be comfortable with this sneaky deception.

More to my liking were the forays onto the college campus in Santa Rosa for the purposes of "witnessing." I loved meeting people and sharing my enthusiasm for the group with them. I had very little chance to witness in this way while I was in the cult. I would say there were not more than a dozen times during my three years in the cult when I was able to participate in this type of activity.

One day, I had gone out with a team of "witnessers" to the campus in Santa Rosa. I had met several interesting people who were very suspicious of what we were doing, when I observed a young man sitting on the lawn reading. I felt very drawn to him, so I went and sat down by him. I engaged him in a friendly conversation, in which I tried to share my life in the group with him without really telling him anything. We were not to mention the Unification Church at all, of course, and we never, under any circumstances, spoke of Moon. We would even deny any connection with them if we were asked about it.

I found out what the young man's interests and ideals were, and proceeded to link them with my ideal life in my community. He listened for quite a long time, and finally he cocked his head to one side and said, "This is really weird, but I feel very compelled to tell you something. I really am not much interested in your community or what you are doing there, but the whole time you have been talking to me I have had the strangest sensation. I know this sounds very strange, but as you have been sitting here, I have had the experience of sitting beside one of the disciples of Jesus Christ. Now I'm not particularly religious, and I can't explain what it means, but I felt greatly compelled to tell you." And he got up and walked away. I just sat there in stunned silence. I could not figure out what it had all meant. Maybe he just had the wrong messiah, but he didn't say a disciple of the messiah, he said a disciple of Jesus Christ. What a strange experience!

In the weeks following, though, I found that whenever I would pray or read, or look at nature, I would feel an overwhelming love for Jesus. I felt great guilt about it, as I knew that I was to love Moon more than anyone, more than life itself, and yet this tremendous love for the gentle, caring, strong, kind, peaceful, compassionate, faithful, patient, truly loving man I had met briefly in my study of the gospels just before learning about the Unification Church was an all-encompassing experience that caught me up into the presence of God in a way that I had never experienced in the cult. I found myself consciously making a great effort to think about Moon when this would happen.

And yet Moon seemed somehow an antithesis of this man Jesus. The implications of this had to be completely subjugated in my mind because of the conditioning of the cult. It was like a reflex reaction to subjugate anything which cast negative thoughts or feelings toward Moon or the organization.

One day I was summoned by Micah and told that I was to be sent to Ukiah on a very important mission that afternoon. I was told to dress up and to fix myself up to look attractive. Micah went on to tell me that we were in great need of some wood to do some improvements. There was a wood mill in Ukiah where we had received some donations before. He went on to say that they had learned the girls were much more successful in obtaining these gifts if they used their feminine wiles on the men in charge. I was told to do everything I could to charm this man into giving us what we wanted.

I was shocked, though I knew that Moon had often told us to use our charms on men to get money while fund raising. Nevertheless, I felt terribly uncomfortable about the whole concept. I did not question what I had been told to do, however, because I was programmed to believe that one never questioned one's "center man." We went to Ukiah, and I did all I could to charm the man, with politeness, winsomeness and some out-and-out flirting.

We came away with our mission accomplished, and I felt depressed about the entire situation. I concluded my negative feelings were just Satan trying to get in my way of doing God's will, so I quickly suppressed these feelings. There were several other incidents when I was called upon to do this same kind of duty to obtain something for the group from the "outside world."

It was becoming more apparent all the time that the "Oakland family" was beginning to trust me. I knew they had been quite suspicious of me because I had spent so much time with the rest of the Unification Church, and there was no great love between the Oakland group and the rest of the organization. I don't think they knew quite what to do with me. I knew too much for them to treat me like a new member, yet I did not really fit into their organization because I had been taught to operate in such a different manner. I expect that Micah had been keeping an eye on me for the entire period. I suspect that I was proving to be trustworthy because I was beginning to be given much more responsibility. I had established a granarium-making enterprise, and had trained others to make the granariums with the highest standards. Because of my hours spent in this granarium-making project, I had become much better acquainted with other members who lived and worked in Boonville.

I was required to attend the prayer conditions late at night with the staff members. We had certain things which were prayed for each night with great intensity, including the induction of certain numbers of new members, the meeting of certain monetary goals, and the conversion of all trainees. These trainees were prayed for by name. There were certain other conditions which were to be brought into being through prayer from time to time, as dictated by national headquarters. The idea behind these prayers was not at all similar to Christian prayer. For example, these prayers were considered to be conditions of indemnity in that they were offerings of our time and energy late at night when we were all exhausted anyway. The prayers were offered on our knees, in a position in which we were bent over to the floor, and often we would go outdoors where the ground was hard and cold and damp. The theory was to make it as difficult as possible so that our hardship would be counted as the payment of indemnity. We were taught that as our prayers rose, God and Satan were both there waiting to claim them. If they were not done just right, with the proper kind of attitude and heart, or if we fell asleep, then Satan would claim the prayer. Because of this, these prayer conditions were very serious business.

The most difficult part of it for me, though, was that I usually had to walk down the empty road in the middle of the night from the children's trailer to the river to meet the rest of the group. These were times of great terror for me, as I was always aware of the presence of evil lurking in the fields and on the road. Often I would catch sight of dark figures darting across the road in front of me, or following me down the hill. I would sing "family" songs all the way down, but it never seemed to do any particular good. Sometimes Stan would walk down with me, and I knew he was experiencing the same things I was, for he would walk so fast that I would practically have to run to keep up. When Abigail joined us for the summer, the three of us would walk down the road just before midnight for the prayers, and we would openly talk about what we saw and heard. It was greatly comforting to me to know that they were seeing and hearing the same things I was, and that it was not just in my head.

One night, as I was returning to the children's trailers alone after the prayer condition, I had a great sense of dread as I was crossing the bridge over the river. I decided to try to analyze the situation, and in doing so, I attempted to concentrate on the beauty of the night. There was a warm, moist breeze blowing inland from the sea, and as I passed a clump of trees, the strong, exotic scent of bay leaves skipped across the breeze. I looked up at the stars sprinkled across the black sky and noticed that there was no moon. As I tried to concentrate on the creation, the sense of terror and dread grew with each step. I attempted to ignore and deny it, but suddenly I saw black shapes closing menacingly all around me. Breathlessly, I began to pray that all my good ancestors would help me, and that God would save me. I began to run, and I became aware of a growing number of other figures around me. These were not dark, but appeared to be human. They accompanied me all the way back to the children's trailers. I cannot help but think that God, in His mercy, sent His angels in a form that I could accept, to accompany me up to the road, because the fear and dread simply melted away with their presence. Even in my state of heresy, God was there to minister to my tremendous need when I called upon Him! And it was His plan to begin moving in a mighty way in my life very soon.

## 11

# Darkness Reigns

*1975*

Summer unfolded in full force, and with it came Abigail and the boys. The days were long and hot, and often we would take the children down to the river and let them have a picnic and swim. Many times Nat would accompany them, and Abigail and I would work in the fields with the work crews from the training session. After the long, hot days, we would sit outside and do work of one type or another after we had put the children to bed.

About that time, Jimmy's mother arrived from New York, saying that she was leaving the group. She took Jimmy and left for Los Angeles to stay with her parents. Pepito was also sent to live permanently with his grandparents. I was so very thankful for his sake, because the torture which he endured there in Boonville was becoming much worse for him. We had even been told to throw the poor little boy into cold water when he screamed hysterically from the inner torture which ate at him all the time. This was done supposedly to remove the evil spirits from him. I hated the whole situation, and was glad to know that he would be in the loving and constant presence of his grandparents from that time on.

Little Jessie, who was then three, was also becoming more and more morose. She would not speak or look me in the eye anymore, and she would just huddle in a corner and stare. I was beginning to be gone much of the time, and could no longer give her the special love and caring I had tried to give her when I was there most of the time.

Just before Abigail arrived, Jessie began setting fires. By that time we had gas hooked up to the small trailer which we used for a kitchen. Jessie would sneak matches, no matter where we hid them, and then would set fires. Several times I caught her hanging over the gas stove, trying to catch herself on fire. On one of these occasions, I was so horrified that I left the children with Deborah and went in search of Micah. When I found him, I told him about Jessie's behavior and confided to him that I was afraid she was possessed. He gave me a long, hard look and said, "Deanna, I think you are just too attached to the children. You have to be tough and righteous, and I think you need to stay here for the weekend and for a week-long training session next week." And that was what I did. Because of my concern and fear for the life of that child, I was separated from the children for over a week, to get my perspective back in the intense indoctrination of the week-long training session.

From that time on, I was put into the training sessions with much greater frequency. In fact, I consistently attended the weekend sessions after Abigail's arrival, and I was usually used as an assistant group leader on these weekends. I was honored and distressed at the same time, for I knew that sometimes after a person had been trained as an *assistant* group leader, he was used as a *group* leader, and that took a total, full-time commitment. Already my own children were beginning to react with the same kind of insecurity and fear that the other children exhibited. I could not even deal with the existence of the problem because it was so painful that I sensed that it could destroy me.

The summer passed in a maze of golden fields, hard work, talking with Abigail and attending training sessions. Our times for sharing were far too few as far as I was concerned. The spiritual activity really increased as the summer progressed, as Abigail and I kept hearing a woman's plaintive voice singing a grief-stricken song about a lost child, and several times we could see dark figures in the fields outside the trailer.

On one particular night, Stan appeared in the door of the trailer wild-eyed and sweating. He told us to come and look outside, and as we stared out the door, I saw legions of these dark figures standing in the fields just staring at the trailer. "There are thousands of them!" Stan gasped. My blood literally ran cold at the sight, and I stood there frozen to the spot. Abigail was the first to recover, and she ran to get the "holy salt." We went completely through both trailers with the ritual and the salt, and yet the oppression did not lift. It was a terrifying night for all of us. Stan later told us that he had been out in the fields plowing on the old tractor when he became aware that he was being watched, yet he tried to ignore it. As he forged onward, the numbers of onlookers grew, as did his panic. Finally he could bear it no more, and he ran to the trailer. The next day he installed spotlights around the trailers which were to be turned on as soon as it got dark.

There were many happy times mixed in with the darkness, as we grew closer. Abigail and I continued to put in long hours helping with the farm work. I really loved working with the earth. One evening I stepped out of the trailer to see the most beautiful sky I had ever seen. The clouds were giving off a soft golden glow as they were washed with gold and pink light. The surrounding hills were a deep golden brown, and the lovely green shades of the trees melted into the golden light. I caught my breath as I took in the beauty around me. Suddenly I was filled with a tender love which brought tears to my eyes as I considered how very much the Father must love us to create such a breathtaking world for us to enjoy. I stood there and cried until the brilliant colors faded into dusk.

As the summer passed, I spent more time than ever in the training sessions. On the weekends, I always functioned as assistant to one of the group leaders, and during this time I developed a great respect and love for these people who were giving everything to their ideal. It was terribly difficult to give up everything for the group the way these leaders were taught to do. It was a matter of subjugating and overcoming all personal needs and desires by sheer willpower. It did not seem to be a matter of really changing people inside, but of blotting out all individuality in favor of conforming to the mold dictated by the group.

This was an often painful and humiliating process, yet a great desire was kindled in me to come to a point of personal sacrifice where I too could give of myself in this manner. It was also a tremendously invigorating experience to go through these training sessions, because there was an incredible energy created by the routine. There was always a rigid program to be followed, and the success of the entire process seemed to hinge upon whether or not the plan was followed perfectly or not. The schedule, the music, the lectures, the attitudes of the cult members, and the group meetings were built upon precise timing. Ironically, there was a great effort to make everything appear to be relaxed and easygoing, but in truth it was anything but these things.

A great deal of the success of these sessions was attributed to the expertise of the cult members in manipulating people from the "outside" with music and group dynamics. There was singing at every opportunity in the schedule, and this singing was a major source of energy and enthusiasm for everyone. I found that I especially fed on these times of group singing as well as on the lectures. I would get "high" in much the same way I had gotten "high" on drugs a few years before. Sometimes it almost built up to a point where I thought everyone would literally explode with energy. It was not a refreshing kind of energy, however, but rather more like the peaking of a surge of Adrenalin.

I found that there was a real art to manipulating the groups. For example, the leader had to have an exact sense of timing, and to know just how and where to lead the discussion after each lecture. He always had to have an answer for every question that was in accordance with the "Divine Principle," or if he did not have an answer, he had to be able deftly to lead the discussion around the question without anyone suspecting that the question had not really been answered. It troubled me that these long-term members of the Oakland group did not seem to have a particularly deep grasp of the entire "Divine Principle," but seemed to have certain aspects of it which they emphasized greatly. I could not argue with their success in recruiting new members though, so I ignored their lack of deep knowledge and understanding of the "Principle."

The more I experienced their training methods, the more impressed I was with their complexity and thoroughness. I found myself anticipating the weekends and beginning to think in terms of what must be accomplished in them.

I could sense that the time was coming when I would literally live my life through these training sessions. It was a feeling of meeting my destiny, and although I could not explain this feeling, it grew stronger with each passing day. In addition, accompanying these feelings was an emotion of great dread, for I knew this would mean the end of my relationship with my children. I had a great fear that terrible things might befall them after I left, but the fear was irrational in the sense that it was greatly out of proportion to the situation. I comforted myself with the knowledge that Deborah would probably be the one to care for the children when I left, yet the thought of being torn away from them was devastating.

The turmoil of these feelings began to eat away at my very being until I thought they would drive me out of my mind. I felt completely torn between my feelings about being part of the training sessions and the devastation of the sacrifice in store when I did. The programming came deeply into play as I considered that this was one of the greatest sacrifices I could ever be asked to make, and it was ultimately the indemnity for my sinful relationship with my ex-husband.

The grief was almost unbearable as I wondered what kind of God would require the sacrifice of innocent children as payment for my sin. They had not done anything wrong, and yet they would suffer the most for my sin. I hated the entire situation, but there was no alternative as far as I knew. In those moments of deep despair, it seemed that it would have been better if I had never had children in the first place. If I had known then what I thought I knew about life and God in those moments of grief, I decided I would never have given the children the burden of life. There seemed to be no way out of the tragedy I had created for those poor helpless children by my sinfulness. I again prayed that I could bear all of the pain and suffering for the three of us.

One sunny afternoon during a training session, I had time to go down by the river and pray in depth. At first the inevitability of the coming separation from my children seemed to overwhelm me, and all I could do was to sob and beg for strength and help. Suddenly the picture of my experience with God before I had come to California flashed back through my mind, and the words of the heavenly Father echoed in my memory. *"You of little faith. Your children have a Father; I am their Father. You must trust me no matter what happens."*

This must be it, the time the Father had known would come. I was touched with tenderness and fear, for I knew now what those words truly meant. I must entrust these children totally to God. For a while I struggled with the greatness of the decision to trust Him. I had seen what had happened to the other children, and I had no reason to believe that anything else could happen to mine, yet the love of my Father lingered in my heart.

Finally, amidst tears of pain, I said, "O Father, these children are truly yours. I soon will have no control at all over what happens to them, and it frightens me more than I can say. I have made my decision. Father, they are yours, I give them to you completely, and they are no longer mine in any way. Father, you can do anything to me you want to, but please take care of them and don't let any evil come on them at all." I felt a terrible finality in what I had done, and knew I could in no way take it back if the children were to survive.

Shortly after that prayer, Abigail and the boys went back to Berkeley for school. I was left with the children and Deborah most of the time, although I spent a great deal of time at the training site doing various chores, sometimes with the granariums and sometimes on the floor of Micah's closet counting the money brought in by the selling teams, and preparing it for deposit.

Micah had a light in his closet, and I could just fit into it under his clothes to sit and count our proceeds. This was a great honor as far as I was concerned, because it meant I had gained Micah's trust. I often sat there doing my work while Micah had the new members in for his pep talks.

The overriding purpose of these particular talks was for Micah to find out what monetary resources the new members possessed, and to talk each new member into turning those resources over to the group.

It was all done very diplomatically. The new members, for the most part, never knew what had happened because Micah somehow gave them the impression that the giving over of their money and possessions was their own idea. It was really quite fascinating to hear these little chats and to observe how Micah was able to achieve his goal with the vast majority of new members with whom he talked.

I was beginning to get a good idea of what had to be

accomplished with each new person. It was a very complex set of manipulations, but when done within the context of the group, it all seemed very natural and right. A deep feeling of belonging to this "family" was beginning to grow within me.

However, along with this sense of belonging came renewed activity in the form of attacks from the forces of evil. For example, on one Friday evening Randi was allowed to come to the children's trailers to visit for a short while. It was early evening, and the rest of the people who had taken part in the week-long training session were cleaning up after working in the fields all afternoon. The schedule on Friday nights included this period of cleaning, followed by a trek to the top of the highest hill on the property, and a festive dinner with songs and individual entertainment, and occasionally, if the group was deemed ready by Micah, a walk up another hill where everyone gathered in a circle to hear Micah reveal Sun Myung Moon to the newer members. This final step was not to be included on that particular night, so Randi had been set free to visit her son and the rest of us for a few minutes.

While she was there, we began a discussion, and although I don't remember what the content of it was, as we talked I began to sense a terribly oppressive presence of evil. Suddenly I was pushed by a strong but unseen force. I gasped, and as I tried to regain my balance, I felt as if someone grabbed me by the throat and began to strangle me. I tried to cry out for help, but couldn't, and was almost immediately thrown down on the floor. Randi and Deborah began to scream and grab at me, but the strength of the force held me tight. Randi began to pray or sing or something. I don't remember if she found the "holy salt" or not, but just when I thought I would surely die, the attack stopped as suddenly as it had begun. I was terrified, of course, and Randi was practically hysterical. She waited to see that I was all right, and then she ran back to the training session trailers.

I pondered the incident and realized that whatever had attacked me was huge and tremendously strong. I immediately thought of the figure which had appeared to me at night several months before. I tried to be calm and to continue the children's schedule as if nothing had happened, but I was terribly shaken.

Before long Randi reappeared at the door of the trailer and said she was to stay with Deborah and the children, and that I was to go down to the main trailer where everyone was having dinner and entertainment. With tremendous relief I set off for the training session.

When Micah saw me enter, he smiled and gave me a knowing look and indicated that I was to join the others on the floor around the low table. Many members and new people were sharing songs and poems they had written about the group or the "Divine Principle" teachings. I settled with great relief into the crowd of happy faces, and felt a sense of protection.

After this incident I spent much more time in the weekly training sessions. This was quite a relief because I had been required to attend late night staff meetings and prayers, which meant I had to walk the winding road in the dead of night, and often alone. It felt good to be amidst all those people, and it somehow gave me a sense of being not as vulnerable. What a trap! Alone I was subject to all sorts of attacks and terror, but with the group I was drawn deeper and deeper into the control that they had over my mind and emotions. In the end, the terror drove me into the arms of the group.

An interesting event occurred about that time. One evening I was summoned by Ira to accompany him to the children's trailers, and as we walked away from the training session, he made a comment to me which nearly broke my heart. He said, "You know I really admire you mothers. I don't see how you bear being torn from your children like you do, it must just tear you apart!" I mumbled something about indemnity, but my heart was so deeply touched by his compassion that it was all I could do not to cry. He continued to tell me that the reason I was needed was that Marie had returned with Jimmy, and that she was supposed to pick up Jessie and take her back to New York with them. I was amazed because just a couple of months ago she had left the group entirely and returned home to Los Angeles. I could not imagine what had happened. Marie told me the story.

Marie recounted that she had been completely disillusioned and had suffered tremendously after she had been sent back to New York several months before, and so had decided she could not bear being in the "family" anymore. At that time she had returned to California to pick up Jimmy at Boonville and to go home to Los Angeles to be with her family.

Upon her return, she found that she had a desperate need to find out the truth about God. Her family was Mormon, and so she went to the bishop of her ward and told him she had been in the Unification Church and had left, but that she had a deep need to know the truth about God. This man immediately put her into some sort of intensive training. She said he told her that it was much the same as the training given to the missionaries of their church. Marie said that the more she heard, the less sense it made to her. She had felt that much of what they were telling her could not possibly be at all scriptural, and that she finally decided that even the "Divine Principle" and the inconsistencies of the Unification Church made more sense than what they were teaching her, and so she called New York and told them that she wanted to come back. They approved her return and told her to come to Boonville and to pick up Jessie and bring her back to New York with her and Jimmy. This was the purpose of her visit to Boonville. I was sad to see Jessie go, but I could only hope that somehow she would be able to see her mother sometimes if she was geographically closer to her.

About this time I had another disturbing experience. I awakened one morning to find that my right knee was swollen tremendously. Since I had never in my life had trouble with my knees, I was unable to think of anything I had done to injure it. The problem turned out to be a very persistent one, and I found that the swelling was accompanied by pain and weakness in my knee. It came to the point where I was no longer able to bear my full weight, and would sometimes fall to the ground for no apparent reason. The problem was interfering with my duties to the point that Micah finally told me to go to the doctor in Ukiah. I was referred by the clinic to an orthopedic surgeon who ran tests and had X-rays taken.

Upon my return following the tests, he told me I had a condition which was not terribly uncommon to the general population. He said that I had been born with my kneecaps off center; although the condition itself was not unheard of, the fact that it was causing these symptoms was quite unusual in a person my age. Apparently most people with the condition have no negative symptoms at all, and in the few who did, it usually occurred in late middle age. He said further that there were several possible therapies which could be applied to correct the condition, but that if they failed, surgery would be necessary, or the problem would become so severe that I would lose the use of my leg.

This whole situation was one of great frustration to me, because I found it very difficult to participate in normal activities, and yet, I had no desire to be laid up in a hospital. I felt it would severely interfere with my growth in the "family." So, I assented to the therapies, which included casting my leg from hip to ankle for a while. I was determined to overcome the entire situation if at all possible.

In the meantime, autumn was tempering the blazing golds of summer with tinges of red and soft yellows. I was spending more time in training sessions than I was with the children, so one warm afternoon when I was caring for the children with Deborah, we decided it would be a good thing to give the children a change of environment because they were tremendously restless. I walked down to the trailers to find Micah and ask him if we could take the children on a picnic. Micah was gone for the afternoon so we found the person who was second in command. She said she thought it was a good idea to take them out, and that one of the farm crew could take us somewhere. I specifically asked her whether we needed to be back at any particular time, and she answered that we could take all the time we wanted.

One of the young men on the farm crew had to run

some errands anyway and offered to take us somewhere and then pick us up later on. We piled all the children into the big truck, and set off to find a place for our picnic. As we drove a few miles out of town and across a river, the young man, Mark, said he knew of a wonderful place a little way further on. He took us to a tree-shaded area beside the river, and next to a grove of redwoods. I was enchanted, so we unloaded the children and arranged a time, three hours later, to meet him in the same spot.

We had a lovely time that afternoon. The children waded in the shallows of the river, and we ate our lunch. Afterwards, we decided to go for a walk in the forest. It was one of the most beautiful areas I had ever seen! The floor of the forest was carpeted with what looked like giant four-leaf clovers and heart-shaped leaves on a vine. The leaves of these plants were about three inches wide, and in the golden pink light filtering through the redwoods, it looked like a fairyland from some story. All I could do was praise God for the beauty of His creation.

We all meandered back to the appointed place in sufficient time to meet Mark, but he didn't come. We waited an hour, thinking he had simply been detained. After an hour and a half, I began to grow uneasy, and finally decided he wasn't coming for some reason.

There we were, in the middle of nowhere with four preschoolers, and it would be dark in an hour or so. I decided that if we stayed where we were, nobody would ever find us, so we set out to find a telephone. The property across the road belonged to one of the large paper companies, and I thought I remembered seeing a visitors' facility off the road, just a short way from us. It took quite a while to walk because the little ones, Dorien and Julie, couldn't keep up and had to be carried. We finally found the facility and a pay telephone outside. Thank the Lord that I had just enough change to make a call.

I reached the training session trailer and gave a message to someone that we needed to be picked up. We hurried back to the meeting place and arrived there just as the sun set. Soon Stan arrived in the big truck.

"Thanks for coming to pick us up. I was afraid we were stuck here," I greeted him.

Stan shot a disgusted look at me and said nothing.

"What happened?" I asked. It was obvious from his expression that Stan was furious about something.

"I would not let Mark come back for you. You had no right to bring the children this far from the farm. It was totally irresponsible," he remonstrated. "You know that they wanted you to oversee the making of the granariums this afternoon. I searched everywhere for you, and you were nowhere to be found!"

I felt great indignation rising within me as I countered his accusation. "I cleared the whole trip with Micah's assistant before we planned anything. Just ask her!" My sense of outrage grew as I continued, "In fact, she was the one who suggested that we bring the children out of town for the picnic."

Stan acted as if I had said nothing at all, and he refused to speak to me all the way back to the farm.

I could not believe that such a situation could exist. It was totally irrational because I had cleared everything with my center person, and had been told I would not be needed for the rest of the afternoon. The more I considered what had happened, the more outraged I became. I had not done anything wrong, and yet I was in trouble. As I wrestled with my emotions, I experienced a change of heart. Stan had intimated that I was really in trouble with Micah, and I knew that since he was my center man, I must humble myself whether I was right or wrong. As I pursued this line of thought it occurred to me that Jesus had been totally unjustly accused and yet he "uttered not a word." A tremendous wave of tender love for Jesus washed over me, and I realized that because Micah was my "Abel," I had to submit to him no matter what. This realization caused me to be filled with a great sense of humility, knowing that there were much greater importances in life than my own self-justification.

I resolved to go straight to Micah and repent of the fact that he felt I had done wrong. Having made this decision, I was overcome with a great sense of peace and humility, and upon our return I set out to find Micah. He had returned and was in his room. When I told his assistant that I needed to see him, she relayed the message to Micah. He immediately summoned me to his room. In tears of repentance, which were honestly felt, I began apologizing and asking his forgiveness. He seemed confused, and so I quickly explained the whole situation. He did not appear to be upset at all, and in fact, he offered his forgiveness immediately and with great tenderness.

I returned to the children with a great belief in the blessings of a contrite heart in any situation. The next couple of weeks contained a brief interlude, during which I was one of the first persons to contract the mumps. The first few of us were immediately sent to our parents to recover in hopes of preventing an epidemic, but the tactic didn't work, because within a week the farm was under quarantine with dozens of cases of mumps. My visit home was quite brief, and there was never any thought on my part of not going back; in fact, I could hardly wait to return to Boonville.

Upon my return, I was immediately planted in the midst of a weekend and a seven-day training session, where I was assigned duties as an assistant group leader. I felt totally renewed and enthusiastic about my commitment to Moon and the group.

Several weeks later, I was summoned by Micah to his room late on a Friday evening. A mixture of dread and excitement filled me as I hurried down the road. My suspicions were confirmed when I spoke to Micah, for he immediately announced that they needed me as a group leader for the week-long training sessions. I was overwhelmed by the prospect, because it was one thing to be an assistant and another altogether to be a group leader! I was afraid I might let Micah and the group down, yet I ached at the opportunity to serve God in that way. I was to report back to the staff trailer as soon as I gathered the things I would need for the session.

As I walked back to the children's trailers to get the things I needed, I was filled with grief. I had known this was coming for weeks, yet it was torturing me to realize I was being taken away from the children for good. All I could do was beg God to take care of them, and try to lose myself in my job. I had found that when I was hurting the most at being separated from the children in the past, it helped if I gave myself completely to the younger members in the groups, because then I was relieved of the tearing edge of the pain, though it never really went away.

I threw myself into my role as group leader with all the dedication I had. There were moments of being totally abandoned to my job, and there were moments of intense pain. One of these occurred one afternoon during the following week when I had taken my group out into the fields to weed for a few hours. I kept them singing "family" songs, and kept the older members sharing inspiring anecdotes about their experiences in the group.

At one point I looked up to see Mark carrying some irrigation pipe down the road and my son, Joshua, was trotting along beside him. My heart cried out, "Flesh of my flesh, heart of my heart," and an overpowering longing to hold him overtook me. I knew better than to act on it since none of the newer members were supposed to know I even had children.

At that moment he caught sight of me, and Mark became aware of the situation. He took Josh's hand and gently led him in the other direction. That wistful, four-year-old face broke into a smile as he caught sight of me, and my heart surely shattered into a million pieces as I raised my hand to wave a greeting. He looked back over his shoulder, and waved his still-dimpled hand in return. It was all I could do to maintain my positive, enthusiastic role as my emotions fought off grief.

I must have done well in my role, for I was rewarded in a most unexpected and intense manner. We had known for weeks that Moon was coming to Berkeley to meet with the "family," but those of us who lived "on the land" did not expect to get to see him. However, I was chosen as one of the few who got to go to Berkeley to hear his talk. I could not believe it! I had not seen him since the "Day of Hope" speech in San Francisco over a year before, and so much had happened since then.

When the time came, we all piled into a van to go to the huge Hearst Street house in Berkeley. I was glad once again to see some of the people I had not seen for a while, including Randi. She had not seen Dorien recently, and I was able to share about him with her. We spent all our time getting the house ready for Moon's visit and witnessing. On a rainy evening the night before Moon's arrival, three of us were witnessing on the streets of the city when we met a young man named Scott. He seemed very interested and I took his name and address, hoping to get him to attend a dinner and a weekend.

I hardly slept that night in anticipation of seeing my messiah the next day. Everyone was wound up to the breaking point, and the excitement was like electricity in the air. We discovered that the "families" from Oregon and some of their surrounding states were coming in for the talk. As we all gathered in the huge rooms of the bottom floor the next evening, I felt an overwhelming pride in the Oakland group. We were by far the largest, most affluent and most powerful group almost anywhere, and not only that, we were also drawing in members at a phenomenal rate. "Father" had to be proud of us too.

Christine began to lead us in chants and songs in honor of our "true parents." The atmosphere was electric as the voices of well over two hundred cult members chanted and boomed. Some people were practically hysterical; it was as if the sound and the tension were hypnotizing everyone.

We were all squeezed together, sitting on the floor. Somehow I ended up sitting at the very front of the group and just a little off to the side. I was ecstatic because I would be so close to "Father."

Finally Moon and his retinue—his interpreter, Colonel Pak, Mrs. Moon (whom we called Mother), and the woman who traveled with her, Mrs. Kim—entered the room. The women sat in chairs behind Moon, and he and Colonel Pak stood before us. Before he began to speak, Moon sat down for a moment while someone else spoke to us. I don't even remember who the individual was because my entire attention and thoughts were focused on Moon. As he sat there I noticed how tired and old he looked. This lasted only for a passing moment, and then his appearance changed abruptly. At that point my attention shifted to "Mother." She had always before dressed in a kimono and wore her hair wound at the nape of her neck in a bun. She had always, because of this, appeared to be the very essence of oriental submission and humility. That night, however, she seemed totally different. Her hair had been cut short in a Western style and she was dressed in a very stylish manner. Her attitude seemed quite changed also. She spoke in what sounded like harsh and annoyed tones to someone. I was shocked and confused, but felt it was not my place to question her behavior.

When Moon arose to talk he thundered and gestured wildly, and spoke in harsh, gutteral tones. Colonel Pak translated all he said, and in contrast he had a mild, calm manner. I found that I was seated practically at "Father's" feet. I could hardly bear the excitement. Moon talked for hours that night, and although I don't remember exactly, it seems as if he talked for approximately five to seven hours. It was tortuous to sit with legs crossed on the floor, unable to move for all that time. I found it particularly painful because of the trouble I had been having with my knee, but I counted the pain as blessing, because it was an opportunity to pay some pretty intense indemnity.

I hung on every word of Moon's talk as if they were the source of life itself, yet I really don't remember much about the content of the talk. It was, generally, an elaboration on Moon's plan to take over the United States and ultimately the world. I was tremendously inspired despite the horrendous pain of sitting with my swollen and aching knee doubled up in front of me.

During the speech, Moon looked directly at me many times. Every look sent a thrill through me, but it was also discomforting because every look seemed to penetrate right through me. I felt as if he knew everything there was to know about me with every look. There also seemed to be more going on than I knew about, because I had the feeling that he was carrying on some type of defiant communication with someone who seemed to be right over my shoulder. There were a couple of times when he looked directly at me and literally sneered at me. I could not understand what was going on, so I tried to ignore the whole situation. At that point in my life, I am quite sure that I would have done pretty much anything he had asked me to do. He could do no wrong in my sight; after all, he was the messiah, the Lord of the Second Advent, and I did not have the ability to look at him or anything else in a rational way.

Moon spoke late into the night and then disappeared quickly upon finishing his speech. I was tremendously inspired by the mission he had laid out that night, and I found it impossible to sleep in anticipation of seeing him briefly the next morning, for he had agreed to come and say goodbye to us early the next day. In my journal I wrote a quick rededication: "I felt, especially at prayer tonight, just how scarred and unworthy I am to have this precious mission. I am *really* determined to succeed for Him (the heavenly Father) and bring Him joy. I love Him *so* desperately!!"

The next morning we all gathered to say farewell to Moon. Everyone was terribly "high," and the excitement in the room was nearly unbearable. Moon played the benevolent father in his remarks and inspired us all to greater determination and sacrifice for the cause before he left. By the time his bodyguards rushed him outdoors and into the waiting limousine, I was very close to hysteria. I felt I had to accomplish whatever was asked of me, no matter what the cost. We returned to Boonville almost immediately to spread the inspiration. Of course it could be shared only with the older members, because the great majority of people up there did not even know who Sun Myung Moon was—at that point in their experience.

I threw myself with renewed energy into my mission, and found myself able to love my group members with a greater maternal love than had been possible before. I loved the training sessions, and knew that the agony of being separated from the children could be borne when I felt I was in the process of helping others come to a true relationship with God. Not only that, the fellowship with other staff members was like heaven for me after the months of relative isolation up by the barn. I also found that all those months of intensive study of the "Divine Principle" were paying off, for there was practically nothing anyone could ask that did not have an answer in the "Principle." I thought it was amazing that the words would just tumble out to match any situation or question. I remember one sunny afternoon in late fall, when I took my group up on the side of a small hill near the trailers to discuss one of the lectures. Other groups were scattered over the surrounding area doing the same thing, and as I surveyed them, a great sense of purpose and contentment flowed through me, and I knew I would be made glad by this ministry of service as long as I was allowed to do it.

There were still tremendously painful times, though. One day during the work period, my group was in the kitchen. For some reason I had to go outside to get something, and as I came down the steps behind the trailer, I saw the children and the woman who was then caring for them coming toward the trailer. Josh squealed out a greeting, and he and Julie and Dorien came running to greet me. I was ecstatic and gave them all a great bear hug. Suddenly I became aware of several people staring at me, among them Micah's assistant. I carefully contained myself, and tried to greet the children enthusiastically, but not too enthusiastically. As the woman caring for them called them away, my heart felt as if it would be destroyed, but I smiled calmly and went about my business. I knew that if I showed any negative effect from this encounter, I would not be able to visit the children at all, but if it appeared that I was unaffected by seeing them, then there would be more of a chance of visiting them sometime.

I think back on how cold and calculated and unemotional I had become, and it is horrifying to me, yet at the time it was a matter of survival. I was learning what was expected of me on a subtle emotional level, and I was also learning to manipulate those expectations of others for my protection. It was very similar to trying to survive in a nightmare in which no one has any morals or compassion, and where common laws of decency do not apply.

The greatest challenge of my life then was working with new people who were "negative," or having problems of some kind. Most people who stayed for the week-long sessions and more extensive training were just sucked into the process of it all. The isolation, the limited sleep, the dietary changes, the intense indoctrination, the implied guilt and fear brought on by the covered and not-so-covered threats of the teachings, and the complete lack of privacy all took their toll. Besides those factors, there was intense mental and emotional manipulation by the leaders. Yet there were always a few who had trouble giving in to it all. It was part of our duty to "work" on these particular people. It was usually determined by the staff what approach would be the most successful, and who could act on that approach the best. Then that person would be assigned to "work on" the new person and report all results. I seemed to be taking on a very maternal identity, though most newer members knew nothing of my children. This role was an acceptable substitution at the time, for the new members were regarded as children.

There was a mounting difficulty for me in my role, however. My knee was getting much worse, and kept me from participation in a complete way. It was becoming more and more a problem, and finally my orthopedic surgeon in Ukiah said that there would have to be surgery. One of the older staff members was a registered nurse, and wanted me to see an orthopedic surgeon in Oakland before I made any hasty decisions. So I was sent to Oakland on the bus, and the new surgeon told me the same thing.

I hated the thought of being disabled in the way I would have to be after the surgery, but I was told that my condition would only become increasingly worse as long as I put the surgery off. It was determined that since the state was paying my doctor bills, I had best go ahead and have the surgery so that I would be able to participate fully.

The prospect of surgery was not the only distasteful matter, for it meant I would have to live in Berkeley at least until the required physical therapy following the surgery was completed. The thought of leaving "the land" was horrifying. I had grown to love the area and the people very deeply, and this would mean I would be torn away from them. Not only that, the greatest burden was that there would be no possibility of even seeing the children. Things were looking very dark, but it was, again, a tremendous opportunity to pay some really heavy indemnity. I knew that there was no choice, for it had been decided for me already.

I had no idea how long it would be before I returned, so it was with a very heavy heart that I climbed the hill to the children's trailer for the last time in the foreseeable future. I had to catch a bus early in the morning, so I was to spend the night at the children's trailer. I was determined to get all the enjoyment possible from the experience with the children. I carefully explained to them what had to be done to me, and why I would be gone for a while, and I tried to just bathe them in enough love to hold them over until I returned. Late that evening, I had to go down to take part in fulfilling a prayer condition, and while I was there, I was summoned into Micah's room, to find that he and his assistant were the only ones in there.

He asked me to sit down near him, so he could talk to me. I sat at his feet, and waited to hear what he had for me. He told me what a good job I had been doing and just how valuable I was to them, and that he was anxious to have me back and able to do all the things I needed to do freely.

Then he got to the heart of the talk. He looked at me and said something similar to, "You have been in the family for very close to three years now. As you know, after three years, you will be eligible for the blessing (the marriage ceremony). However, as long as you have the children from your fallen marriage, you cannot be blessed. Now I know that the heavenly Father wants to have you blessed in a true marriage with true children, but in order for that to happen, you will have to get rid of your fallen children. So you had better start thinking about how you can get your ex-husband or your parents to take them for good. I know you will pray about this and come to a decision while you are recuperating." He went on to assure me how much God and the "family" loved me and to send me on my way with his blessings.

I smiled, and nodded cheerfully, and left the room, but it was as if my mind and my emotions had slammed shut with a resounding bang. I could only send up a fleeting plea, "O Father, please protect them!" To deal with what had just happened, in any emotional sense, was utterly impossible, for it would have been completely destructive. By not allowing myself to feel anything at all, I was protecting the children, for if I had fallen apart, there would never have been a chance for me to see them again. This way, by subjugating my natural reactions, there was at least a door open. I was completely torn, for the blessing was everyone's goal, and one was not really saved in any way until it had been accomplished. At the moment, however, I could only put the demand on "hold" until after the surgery.

It was with almost unbearable pain that I held and soothed my children that night. I could sense that Joshua had great misgivings about the surgery and the fact that I was to be so very far away for an undetermined period of time, and underneath the veneer of assurance that I showed to them, I felt nothing but terror. I sensed that somehow this was the end of an era, that nothing would ever be the same again. As the bus departed from the station and headed for San Francisco the next morning, I felt desolation which threatened to overcome me entirely. All I could do was to beg God for mercy, yet at the same time, I wasn't at all sure anymore that God had any mercy to give.

## 12

# The Battle Explodes

I arrived in San Francisco with a feeling of complete desolation. From the San Francisco station I had to walk to another bus terminal where I was to catch a bus for Berkeley. Everywhere I looked I saw evidence of pain and sin; the world seemed to be more evil than I had ever perceived it before, and I sank even deeper into a feeling of sorrow and hopelessness. The only way out, I thought, was to suffer enough to be set free, and I could see that I had all the opportunity for suffering I could ever want. Possibly, much of it could be paid off very quickly if it didn't destroy me first.

After arriving in Berkeley, I walked to the smaller house which the "family" owned, for there I was to meet Shirley, the girl who was a nurse, and she was to take me to the hospital. As we drove to the hospital, I spoke with her about my feeling that because I was able to give the love I had given to my children to the new recruits, the pain of my separation from my own children was not as great. I said that if I could work with the recruits this way, I felt I could make the sacrifice I had been ordered to make. I truly felt I had no choice, and that if giving the children up now meant salvation for them later, then it was the only choice.

It seemed strange that when I registered at the

hospital, Shirley did not register my parents as being my closest relatives, but gave only names of cult members. It was as if my personal identity did not exist anymore, and that the only identity I had was that of a member of a group. I didn't question it at the time, but it was very indicative of my situation.

That evening, the anesthesiologist came in to determine what he would do for the surgery on my knee. He checked me thoroughly and said he did not dare to put me under a general anesthetic because my physical condition was so very poor. He said that for one thing, I had a severe case of bronchitis, in addition to being terribly run down. I was surprised because I had been feeling quite well compared to the way I had felt in general for the last two years. I mused that if the doctor thought I was bad now, he should have seen me in the preceding months. Because of my condition, it was determined that a spinal block would have to be used so as not to jeopardize my ability to breathe.

The night before the surgery I experienced much fear. It occurred to me that if something happened to me, no one would ever know, except the cult members, and who knows whether they would even tell my physical family. I decided I had better call my natural parents, and when I did, it was comforting to talk to my mother, for she was very concerned and said she would pray for my safety. I knew that as far as the cult members were concerned, I might as well be dead for the time I was away, and I knew there would be no supplications for my safety from them, because I was just at the mercy of the indemnity I had to pay. In other words, until I returned, I was of no use to them, so in a very real sense I ceased to exist for them.

Early the next morning I was given something to

make me sleep, which had the effect of making me feel as if the walls were closing in on me. I fought the sleep with all my might, for I was filled with fear, and it became very real to me that I was totally in the hands of God. Normally this surgery would not be a threat, but with my terrible physical condition, I felt very vulnerable. At that time I realized I did not trust the God I had seen operating in the Unification Church, for the fruit of his presence was totally merciless. Certainly, I was chosen to do this work for the new messiah, and because of this, I was supposed to be protected. But I also knew of others who were supposed to have been protected and who had died violent deaths. I cried out to God in my fear, but the fear and extreme loneliness did not diminish. Finally, the drug won out, and I fell into a deep sleep.

The surgery was a great success, but for three days I was kept drugged to the point of incoherence. As I began to be aware of my surroundings, I realized that I was no longer alone in the room, for there was an older lady in the bed across from me. It turned out that she had recently had cancer surgery and had remained in the hospital to begin chemotherapy treatments. She was a bright, personable woman, and her husband was kind and caring. For me, it was wonderful to have someone to care for and to talk with. She asked me about myself, and I found that I was very uncomfortable telling her anything. I'm sure she could not understand why I did not have any family there, and especially why no one in this group I had given my life to ever came to see me or even called to see how I was doing. She and her husband felt sorry for me, I'm certain, and spent many hours sharing with me and trying to show that they cared for me even if no one else in California did. It was a great help to me that my mother called nearly every day, and for that short time, I began to feel as if I were not really alone to face and fight an evil, hostile world.

The day I had to go home was very traumatic. First of all, no one arrived to get me, so I called the center and found that they had forgotten all about me. There was a man named Zechariah at the center, and he said he would come and pick me up. Again, the feeling of intense desolation which had washed over my time with the group took hold of me. I found to my extreme dismay that I was crying when I bid the older couple goodbye, because it was so difficult to give up their caring and compassion.

I found that I was to stay at the big, main house in Berkeley. I had rather hoped I would go to the smaller house because it would be so much easier for me to get around after my surgery. I was in a cast from my hip to my toes, and had been told to stay off my leg completely for at least a week, and then I was to restrict my activity very carefully. The doctor emphasized that I must care for myself strictly or my leg would not heal properly, and I would have more trouble than before.

When I arrived at the big house, I realized I would be required to face three flights of stairs several times a day. My physical condition was very bad, for they had not been able to clear up the bronchitis while I was in the hospital. In addition, I had lost quite a bit of blood, and the doctor said it would take awhile to regain my strength. I knew, however, that those things would not matter, because I was just a cog in the wheel, and my personal needs had to be completely subjugated to the purpose of the whole.

I struggled up three flights of stairs to deposit my things in the girls' quarters. During my recovery I was to be a group assistant to a staff member named Edie. I had always liked her very much, and had assisted her several times in Boonville the previous summer. Of all the group leaders, I suppose I was glad I had been assigned to her, for there was still a remnant of gentleness and concern in her.

I found that I was expected to comply with the general schedule, which meant that I was allowed to have as much as five hours of sleep a night. It also meant attacking those three flights of stairs several times a day. Because I was not able to keep up with the other individuals who were working on the streets, it was decided that I would be assigned to answer the telephone in the center during the day. The newspaper had recently exposed us as members of the Unification Church, and it was my job to take all the resultant calls. These ranged from people calling to harass, to hysterical parents, to concerned citizens who felt an obligation to call and tell me about all the evil things our leader and the group had perpetrated on the public. But since I had been programmed to believe that all negativity about the group was from Satan, none of the allegations affected me at all.

My bronchitis continued to get worse, and finally the powers in control of the center decided that I should go to a doctor. It was Zechariah who was assigned to drive me, which delighted me, because he and I were friends. He had a book which he took along to read while he waited for me. I could not imagine where he had gotten it, and I asked him about it. He said it was a book about the Scriptures pertaining to the end times and that it was fascinating and quite disturbing. After my appointment, we began to discuss the book again. He said a very strange thing to me. "You know," he mused, "sometimes I think I'm really in the wrong place."

I was distressed, and asked him why in the world he thought that.

"Well, I was a Christian when I joined this group, and the reason I joined is because I was looking for some really moral people to fellowship with. I found that you people were about as moral as anyone I had met, so I moved in."

That was true, I thought.

He broke into my thoughts again by saying, "But, the more I hear the more I doubt what's going on here."

I felt confused. "But why?" I asked.

"You see," he continued, "Jesus Christ was my King, and I'll tell you right now, Jesus Christ will always be my King, and I mean forever. Nothing your 'Divine Principle' says will ever change that!"

I was stunned. I felt like I should say something in defense, but for some reason I was unable to think of anything, or to get anything out of my mouth. We returned to the center in silence.

I found that disturbing things were happening to me; for example, I was unable to read the "Principle" or any of the "Master Speaks" which belonged to me. They just didn't make sense. In addition, staying in the center throughout the day was terribly depressing. There was a great oppression which hung like a heavy blanket over the house. It manifested itself in a heavy, dark presence that covered everything. It seemed to be diminished somewhat when everyone came home, and there was much activity, but nevertheless I sank into a deep, dark depression.

Physically, I was no better, and I began to have pain in my leg, and periods of feeling faint. Yet, I was caught between two opposing forces. Every time Shirley came to the house, she admonished me for not taking care of myself, and threatened me with all the things the doctor had told me. She told the staff that I was not to go up and down the stairs and was to get plenty of rest. But after she left, it was made very clear to me that I was expected to do everything everyone else did, except to go out on the streets. The center director gave me hostile looks every time I had difficulty keeping up, and I felt that she was judging me each time I felt weak or sick. Several months before, she had broken her foot or her leg and had overcome by forging onward; I was to do the same thing because it was just selfishness to allow it to get in my way. It never seemed to occur to her that major surgery was not the same thing as a simple fracture. It made no difference that the whole structure of my knee had been changed, and had to heal in just the right way, or the surgery would have to be redone, with much less chance of success. These factors did not even enter into her perception of what was happening to me, and as nearly as I could tell, I was just an irritation to her because of my condition. It was all very disheartening and I tried to push onward, but I felt as if I were losing ground every day, because each day it was more and more of a struggle to go on.

Then one day, I experienced a great trauma. Randi had come down to Berkeley after having spent a week on the farm. She took me aside and said, "Did you know that they're leaving the children alone up there all day long?"

I just stared at her. "What do you mean?" I asked.

"Well, they feed them and dress them, and then they leave them alone for hours at a time."

I was stunned, and felt as if I had been slapped in the face! How could they leave a four-year-old alone with two two-year-olds in that way? I could not comprehend it.

"Well, something has to be done!" she continued. "I just wish I knew what I could do with Dorien to get him out of there."

I stared blankly at her. "I just don't understand how they can treat those little children like that," I whispered.

"Oh, it's not their fault," Randi asserted, "the kids are just in their way up there. If I could just think of somewhere to send Dorien where he would be accepted, I'd do it in a minute!"

I stared at her, suddenly comprehending that the work of transformation had been done in her. They had killed all compassion and decency in her and turned her into a block of ice. They had literally murdered the parental love in her. In shock and disgust I turned and walked away from her. Hysteria welled up in me as I headed down the stairs to the den where I had been answering the telephone all day. As I entered the room, I grabbed the telephone in desperation and called the smaller house in Berkeley where Abigail was living with the older boys. When she came to the phone, I recounted what was happening to the little children up in Boonville. "What can we do for them?" I begged. There was a silence. Finally Abigail answered. "There isn't anything to be done. All of this pain you think you're feeling, it isn't real. If you chant and pray real hard, it will all go away, and you'll find that you weren't really feeling it in the first place. It's all just a trick of Satan to try to bring you down." She then said goodbye and hung up. I was in a daze. It was all like the nightmares I had had since childhood, of being in the control of and at the mercy of a force or group that was completely ruthless. The nightmare was a reality! I felt as if I could do nothing in the face of it all, so I began to chant and pray. The horror was relieved somewhat, but I had the sensation of being hopelessly caught in a spider's web.

I threw myself completely into my chores to alleviate the growing sense of dread. While I had been at the Hearst Street house in Berkeley, I had determined to try to get Scott, the young man we had met witnessing the night before Moon's arrival, into the group. I called him and invited him to dinner at the center. He came gladly, but according to the center director, he was the most difficult person she had ever tried to lecture. He kept asking questions, and refuting what she was saying. But I did not give up on him. He was a really good person, and I was determined that he was chosen by God. He often came to see me, and even took me to lunch one bright November afternoon when practically everyone else was in Boonville. It was a strange afternoon, for I talked incessantly about the group and its ideals, and all he wanted to talk about was me. I realized how totally opposed to society the group was, and I had a fleeting sense of longing for some sort of normality in my life. But by the end of the afternoon, I had determined that he was interested in me, not the group, and that although he was a beautiful, kind, caring individual, he was not material for the group.

I felt so horribly alone. It seemed a tremendous paradox to me that in the midst of all those people, I could be so totally alone. But, some relief seemed to be in sight because one of our great celebrations was close at hand. We did not celebrate any of the Christian holidays, but had our own, and one of these was about to arrive. I knew that many of the members from Boonville would be coming down for it, and my heart filled with anticipation.

As the day drew near, tremendous preparations took place. We cleaned the house from top to bottom, and prepared great culinary delights. These holidays provided the only opportunity for us to eat anything but variations of rice and some vegetables. The morning of the celebration arrived, and we were all up at four-thirty. We had the special ceremony which was normally reserved for Sundays at 5:00 A.M., in which we dedicated ourselves to God and Moon and recited a pledge of our allegiance. Then the preparations for the celebration were completed. All the members from the three houses in Berkeley, and the one in San Francisco, arrived. The older members chosen to attend from Boonville also arrived, and I could hardly contain myself. It was so good to see them again, and I felt a sense of belonging which I had missed dreadfully for weeks.

During the ceremony, we had to stand in rows, girls on one side of the room, and men on the other. As I stood there I began to feel faint. I started to have a blackout, and one of the sisters grabbed me. She said that I looked like death, I was so pale, and I had broken out in a cold sweat. One of the staff members saw what happened, and told some of the other members to take me into the den, where I could lie on the couch for a while. I was filled with terrible guilt at having to leave the ceremony.

As I lay there, a terrible frustration at my physical

condition overcame me. Shirley came in and told me to stay exactly where I was, and that she would have food sent in to me. She scolded me for not taking care of myself, and said that my weakness and the pain in my knee were the direct result of my abusing myself. After she left, our center director came in to use the telephone. She glared at me and pointedly ignored my presence. I had the strong sense that she was totally disgusted with my physical weakness, and wanted no part of me until I overcame it. I felt totally miserable as I realized that no matter what I did, it would be wrong.

Later on, Shirley came and told me I could get up. I attended the festivities, which included entertainment by various "family" members. At one point, Dr. Dirks, who was of Jewish lineage, got up and began to sing in Hebrew and to do a Hebrew folk dance. He summoned other young men who were also of Jewish lineage, and soon there were at least a dozen young men dancing in a circle and singing in Hebrew. As I watched and listened, the presence of the Almighty God became manifest to me, and I was filled with a tremendous love for and longing about the Jewish people. I felt the love and longing of God himself for them, and I was overcome with God's immediate presence. I contemplated what it could mean, for we had been taught that God had forsaken the Jewish nation forever. Yet, how did this fit into what I was experiencing? I had so seldom felt the presence of the Lord since I had joined the cult—it was like a blinding light. I could not understand what it all meant.

Later that day, I had gone upstairs. As I came out of our room, Micah was coming down the hall. He grinned at me and said how much they missed me up in Boonville. I asked him if I could come back, and he said that they really needed me to come back as a group leader, but that it was up to the powers in Berkeley as to when and if I could come back, and he reminded me that I could not return until my therapy was finished.

My heart sank as I realized that my fate was in the hands of the center director there, and that she didn't even like me in the first place, and reputedly had no mercy at all. My heart sank.

Soon afterwards, I was sitting in the den on telephone duty. As I sat there, I became aware of loud voices coming down the stairs. As they approached, I realized that one voice belonged to one of the staff members, and the other was that of another member. The staff member was yelling at the other girl, and that girl was crying and pleading about something. The din grew louder as they came down the stairs, and finally I heard a loud slap. I knew that the staff member had slapped the younger member. In that instant, out of nowhere, the thought which came to me was, "Would Jesus Christ have slapped His followers like that?" I felt myself become breathless as I struggled to come up with an answer. If I would have said, "Yes, Jesus would have done that," then I was clearly lying; yet if I said, "No, He wouldn't have slapped His followers," it meant there was definitely something wrong in the group, for it was not at all unheard of for one of the staff members to use physical violence on the other members. I had heard of incidents of this sort everywhere I had been in the Unification Church. I had been programmed to believe that any negative implications about the group were from Satan, so it was a real mental dilemma! I finally decided that I didn't have to answer the question at all.

My depression deepened as the days dragged by, and my physical condition was going rapidly downhill. I decided that what I needed was to pay a bit of heavy indemnity. I had been in the cult for about three years at that time, but I had never been allowed to do the seven-day water fast which was required of all members sometime within the first three years. Out of desperation, I asked Edie if I could do it. She asked the center director, and it was approved. The date was set on which I would begin the fast, and I felt anxious to have the chance to pay the indemnity. Maybe it would break me out of the terrible depression which had settled over me during the past few weeks.

Meanwhile, one evening on a weekend, my family called. My grandparents offered to pay for tickets both ways if I would bring the children and come home for Christmas. I immediately told them I could not, and said I just had too many responsibilities. In actuality, we had been told that no one was to go home, because parents had mounted an active campaign to get their children out of the cult. I knew that any request would be denied immediately. But my grandparents were terribly insistent. Then my parents called and put more pressure on me. When I gave them the same story, my father became obviously upset, and they would not hang up until I promised to at least ask. I felt trapped, but made the promise. Most of the cult members were in Boonville for the weekend, and the only staff members in town were at the Dirks' house, so I called there. It was Shirley who answered the telephone, and I poured my story out to her. Suddenly I heard a voice on the extension phone. It was the Korean woman who headed up our group. She said something to the effect, "So your parents called and want you to come home for Christmas?"

"Yes, they did."

"Was your father really mad when you told him no?"

"Yes he was."

"What does your father do again?"

"Well," I answered, "he's an attorney." There was a silence.

Then she said, "I think you had better go home for a week and calm him down; he could cause us trouble."

"But they want me to bring my children," I said.

"All right then, take them, but I want you back here in a week. Goodbye."

I was stunned; I felt like she had told me to jump into the lion's den. I was a mess anyway, the depression and constant feelings of fear were becoming more and more magnified each day. I could only hope that I could pay enough indemnity to overcome these things before I got to my parents' house, for I felt that when I arrived there I would be fighting in Satan's territory.

There was another problem. I felt that unless I had physical possession of the children, they would never be brought down from Boonville to go with me, yet I could think of no way for me to get up there to get them. I asked the center director if I could go up, and she said absolutely not, citing my physical condition as the reason. I felt defeated, for it was beginning to occur to me that this might be the answer to getting the children to safety. I prayed that if this were true, that God would have my mother offer to keep them. But first I had to get them to her.

Within several days, a letter arrived, stating that I had to come to Mendocino County to sign some legal papers—or my check for the children, which they had never had access to, would be cut off. I showed the letter to the center director, and she ordered me to go to Boonville and sign the papers.

I was totally amazed by the whole situation. Things seemed to be happening so fast. Meanwhile I had decided that I had better start my fast. I picked a night and had it approved. That night after the newer members had gone to bed, I showered, and dressed nicely, and went to the prayer room to set the condition for my indemnity. The purpose of this particular fast was to pay the indemnity for a release from Satan. I prayed the ritual prayers, asking the heavenly Father to accept the indemnity of a seven-day water fast as the condition for a release from Satan. It was a tremendously appropriate time to be doing such a fast, for I had been feeling the presence of Satan in my life in a new and powerful way, and I wanted more than anything to be rid of it. I wept tears of humility as I realized that only God could set me free through the condition I was setting that night, and I entered into the fast with a tremendous sense of anticipation.

The evening of the day the letter arrived from the county, I was loaded into a van which was headed for Boonville. My plane, the tickets for which had been obtained miraculously by my grandparents in Utah when there were absolutely no reservations open in San Francisco, was to depart in two days. I would have just enough time to go to Ukiah and sign the papers, and catch a ride back to Berkeley with the children the next day so we could catch the plane at six o'clock the following morning.

It was late at night when we set out for Boonville, and we arrived at about three o'clock the following morning. Because I was not going to be a part of the training session, I had to stay at the trailer where the children were kept, up by the barn. I was let out there, and I struggled with my crutches across the frosty and slippery grass to the trailer where I knew the children would be sleeping. After much difficulty, I got into the door where the steps were. It was pitch dark, so I felt my way down the hall to where the children slept. The whole hallway was blocked off with boxes. I called out to the girl who was staying with them. She called back, saying they had blocked off the hall so that the health inspector would not know we had hooked an extra bathroom up to the septic tank which had finally been installed for the other little trailer. I groped my way around to the other door. It was terribly cold, and as I dragged myself up through the other door, I realized that the heavy fog was settling into frost on the floor of the trailer. I asked her where my children were, and she pointed their dark forms out to me on the floor. Joshua was huddled into the end of a sleeping bag, but Julie was merely wrapped in a thin blanket, lying on the bare floor. I grabbed her and held her to me as I sat on the frosty floor, and found that she was shivering so terribly that I could hardly hold onto her. I wrapped the blanket around us both, covering our heads so that our breath would help to warm us. As I sat there clutching her, the most awful dread and fear came over me. I felt as if death itself was beside me, and I felt a terrible sense of threat against the children. I sat in terror, holding my baby for the rest of the night.

At the break of dawn, I packed the children's few, ragged things and caught a ride in a car in which some of the other members were returning to Berkeley. On our way, we went through Ukiah so I could sign the papers to obtain child support for the children, so the cult would continue receiving the checks.

When we arrived in Berkeley, the children and I were dropped off at the smaller house to spend the night. It was good to see Abigail again, and it soothed my fear. I was into the fourth day of my fast, and was feeling somewhat lightheaded and disoriented, but being with Abigail helped. Most of the other members were working in a delicatessen owned by the group, so we had some time to talk as we worked in the house. Toward the afternoon, one of the young men whom I had seen come into the group when I was in Boonville came in. It turned out that he had been asked to help start an elementary school for the group. We began to talk, and I revealed that I only had one semester to finish before graduation with a degree in education when I had joined the group. He spoke of his plans, and I got quite excited. Maybe this was what the heavenly Father had in mind for me all along. I would love to finish school and be a teacher, with the opportunity of being with and helping children. We discussed the plans for some time, and as we talked, I felt my enthusiasm rekindled and my hope growing also.

As it got later that afternoon, other members came in from time to time, and many of them were people I had come to know when I was in Boonville. I began feeling a deep sense of belonging again, something I had not felt much in the Hearst Street house.

Sometime during the early evening I had quite a surprise. The doorbell rang and it was Scott, the young man I had worked with, but had given up on. He looked very upset, and asked to speak with me alone. I asked him what was the matter, and he poured out his distress.

He asked me why I hadn't ever mentioned my

children to him.

I couldn't tell him that I had been trained not to speak of them, so I mumbled something about the fact that I had thought it was unimportant.

He stared at me with uncomprehension. "How could your own children be unimportant?" he gasped.

I had no answer. I told him that I was headed for Colorado for a week, but that I would be back.

He asked me if I was going to take the children, and when I said that I was, he looked relieved. He proceeded to say that he had tried to contact me at the Hearst Street house, and had been told that I was at the smaller house with my children. His tone of voice sounded like an accusation. Again he asked how I could have known him that long, and spent time with him at the center, without mentioning the fact that I had children.

Again I had no answer.

He shot me a look of hurt and frustration, and said that he just couldn't understand my attitude about my own children, and he turned and left.

Confusion and guilt overcame me. Had I done something wrong? I knew I had done only what I had been taught to do, so I let the matter drop. I just could not deal with Scott's emotional shock and outrage at my attitude and actions in terms of what I knew about my struggle to have a "right" attitude in the eyes of the cult.

We put all the children to bed, and shortly thereafter Christine came over. Among other things, she took me aside to get my parents' names, address, and phone number. She also confirmed my return reservations, and said that she would see me in a week. She told me to do a good job of placating my father before I returned, and said goodbye. A sense of urgency was growing in me, and the sense of feeling terribly threatened by some of the staff members came back.

I knew that Edie was to take me to the airport before 6:00 A.M., yet I had all kinds of fears that she wouldn't show up. I sat awake all night, watching the children to make sure that nobody took them, and pondering the evil of my situation. I felt sure that my fear was from Satan, so I prayed and sang softly for hours. Then it occurred to me that my situation at my parents' was no better. What if they tried to restrain me? They had never tried anything before, but I had a sense of ominous threat. I decided that it was worth the chance if it meant getting the children to safety.

Before dawn the next morning, Edie arrived to drive us to the airport outside San Francisco. I liked Edie a lot, and we had a good talk. I left with the determination to "fight it out" at my parents' home, but I was, for some unfathomed reason, greatly relieved when Edie walked out the door to return to the center.

It was an arduous trip back to Colorado, for I was still in the cast from my hip to my toes, plus I was in the fifth day of my water fast, so I was quite weak. The airline people were a great help, and when we landed in Salt Lake City to change planes, my grandparents, who were paying for the trip, met me and helped me get the children and myself to the other plane. They were going to drive to Colorado later on.

The children were fed well on the plane, for which I was ecstatic, and they both fell asleep during the last leg of our journey. I was left with my thoughts and my prayers. Mixed feelings came over me as I realized that this might be the last time I would ever travel anywhere with them. Yet I prayed fervently that if the heavenly Father wanted them with my parents, that He would put it into my mother's heart to offer to keep them.

As we finally began to circle the airport in Montrose, I began to cry quietly. In my confusion of feelings, I didn't even know why I was crying. As I was helped off the plane, I caught sight of my loving family waiting for us, and again, a deep sense of fear and dread crept over me.

## 13

# *Advent of the King*

Once we arrived at my parents' house, and I had put our things into the rooms where we were to stay, I felt a sense of relief. It was as if a tremendous pressure had been lifted from me, although I remember being very reticent, not feeling at all free to share my thoughts or emotions with my family. It was terribly difficult to appear normal with all the burdens I had on my heart, but the children were ecstatic to be with my family again. I am sure that they received more loving attention that evening than they had received in all the months we had been separated.

That night when everyone else was in bed, I went downstairs to my room. For some reason, I opened the bottom drawer of the dresser and found, lying on top of everything else, an old picture of my grandmother who had died when I was an adolescent. I picked up the picture, and I remember her gentle love for me, and in doing so, I felt pierced to the heart. I began to weep and grieve at the abuse my children had experienced recently. As I did so, I began to moan, and whisper, "What kind of a God are you, to require the sacrifice of innocent children to achieve your purpose?" An intense sense of stillness crept over the room, and I suddenly felt as if someone were sitting next to me on the floor. This presence cradled me in its arms, and I remember rocking back and forth as if I were a small child in the loving arms of a parent. In the quiet I heard, *"It's all right, everything will be all right; God is not like that."* In complete exhaustion I fell asleep on the floor, and barely remember climbing into bed much later.

At first I was so wound up that I could hardly sleep. I tried rigorously to adhere as much to the basic schedule of the center as I could. I was not at all able simply to sit still, but felt the compulsion to be doing something constantly when I was awake, so I began to do some baking for Christmas. I was still on the seven-day water fast, but I felt no desire at all to eat. My mother was appalled by the fact that I was fasting in my physical condition, although I told her that I had just started the fast on the day I arrived at their house. I was absolutely determined to keep the condition of indemnity I had set, because more than anything else, I wanted to be set free from Satan's influence.

I found that it was terribly difficult to hold and nurture my children. I kept thinking that this might be the last time I would be with them, and I felt it would be easier on them if I did not let them get too attached to me before I went back. It was literally torture to have Julie climb into my lap and snuggle down, knowing what I did about having to give her up, and sometimes I would have to go and lock myself in the bathroom and cry into a towel to relieve my agony.

It was a lovely Christmas, and we all attended the midnight worship service together. I was touched by it, but felt sad that no one else knew the whole truth as I thought I did. I truly cried out to God on that night, in the gentle atmosphere of Jesus' presence. I only wanted to do what God wanted me to do before it destroyed me.

By Christmas both of the children were sick. Joshua developed a severe ear infection, and I had to take him to a doctor. I was told that he must take antibiotics, and that he could not possibly travel on an airplane until the infection was gone. I was confused, for my mother had not offered to keep the children, and so possibly I was supposed to take them back after all. The thought of returning them to the torture they had endured tore me apart, but I called the center in Berkeley and told them the situation. They agreed that I had best reschedule my return, but as soon as was possible.

I called the airline and rescheduled my flight for a week later, and settled in to wait. Meanwhile, I had finished my seven-day fast as I had been determined to do, and yet, instead of the presence of evil being dispersed, it seemed worse than ever. I found that on most nights I would awaken in a cold sweat with awful fear and terror filling me and the room. My days were no longer bearable, for they too were filled with this presence of impending doom. In addition, there was no one to reach out to, because I did not trust my family and I felt they could not possibly understand what I was experiencing; besides, Satan was probably using them against me. There was no priest at my parents' church, for their priest had left, and no one had come to replace him yet.

My friends from times past seemed inane and silly in their concerns, and I felt that they were operating from a worldly realm primarily, and could not even begin to grasp the struggle for eternal life which was engulfing me. In other words, I had never felt so abandoned and alone in my entire life, and I prayed almost constantly in my mind for God to show me what I was supposed to do. I could hardly bear to have a civil conversation with my family; I wanted to scream and moan and wail and pour out my distress, but I knew they would think I was crazy. Consequently, in my despair and frustration, I became hostile, and angry and rude. It was all I could do to be at all civil, and most of the time I had to fake congeniality for the sake of those around me.

Before I had to leave, during my second week at home, my mother came to me and asked if she and my father could keep my children and raise them. I was both terribly relieved and saddened, for I felt that this was the answer I had been looking for. I was relieved that the children would be well cared for, and above all, loved, but I also knew that this meant I might never see them again. Engulfed by these thoughts, I cried all that night.

I received a phone call from the airline shortly thereafter saying that they had overbooked my flight, and that I could not get another reservation for approximately two weeks. I called the center in Berkeley again with the distressing news, and they were terribly upset—until I told them that I would be leaving the children with my parents in Colorado. This seemed to be a tremendously calming factor, and they seemed very supportive and encouraging in my dilemma after that; in fact, they promised to call and give me news and moral support until I could get back.

In the days following, I found that I was hardly able to sleep at all. My mind was whirling with confusion, and the more I considered my situation, the more I felt that maybe I was not to return to the Oakland group at all. My "spiritual mother," Mary, had been sent to the continent of Africa as a missionary, so I could not contact her. Also, I found that although there were many members in the Oakland group whom I loved very much, I hated the deception more than ever. If I was going to give up my children permanently, then I wanted to devote myself to an intense and open following of the man I thought to be the new messiah. I could easily call the group in Colorado and plead my case, because I had met the state director when I was in Wyoming, and felt he would possibly understand my convictions about lying concerning my devotion to Moon. I knew that in all likelihood I would be sent back to New York, but my location made little difference, since no matter what happened, I would be separated completely from my physical family. At least this way I could openly claim my devotion to Moon.

The sense of evil surrounding me grew more and more apparent as the days passed. Finally, one night I awoke suddenly with my heart pounding and my palms sweating, and as I peered into the darkness, I saw that the room was filled with dark figures, crowding all around my bed. The terror was so extreme that I thought I would surely die right there. I could not utter a word. The songs and the "holy salt" were completely useless that night, and a terrible grief and despair overcame me. I knew I could not endure this kind of thing any longer, yet how could I get away from it? I also knew I could not take my own life, for that was a great sin, yet I had no will to continue to live. I finally decided that the only way out would have been if I had never existed at all, and so I began to grieve that I had ever been given life.

Suddenly, I could hear the dark, hideous figures laughing at me and taunting me, and I realized that this must be what hell is like. Instantly, I knew that no matter what happened, I would do what God wanted me to do, for I knew I could not endure this separation, aloneness, terror and revulsion for one moment longer, and certainly not after I died.

I scrambled out of bed as fast as I could and fell upon the floor, face down. I heard myself call out to God in a desperate whisper, "O my God, I don't even know who you are! Are you cruel and uncaring and vindictive? Are you loving and caring? Are you the God I learned about in Sunday school when I was growing up, or are you the God of the Unification Church?" Suddenly I knew that they were not the same. "I will do anything you ever ask me to do if you will only tell me who you are, and what you want me to do!" I stopped, and an overwhelming hopelessness came over me.

There was no one I could trust to tell me the truth. I couldn't trust my family or friends, and I now knew I did not trust anyone in the Unification Church. My prayer seemed hopeless, and I had begun to weep, when I had a sudden thought. There was one person I could trust, because even in the Unification Church we were taught that the man Jesus is sinless and perfect. Therefore, He couldn't and wouldn't lie to me. So, praying again, I said, "Jesus, who is the King? Is it Sun Myung Moon, or are you the King?" I didn't know how to end the prayer, because for over three years I had not ended a prayer with anything other than "In the names of the true parents," but somehow this didn't seem right. I decided that if I was going to ask Jesus, I'd best pray in His name. So I finished, "Jesus, please show me the ultimate and whole truth. In Jesus' name I pray, Amen."

A tremendous peace crept over me, and I fell asleep,

and had the first night of restful sleep that I could remember. This peace filtered into the next morning, but by afternoon the feeling of confusion had returned. I just kept clinging to the knowledge that Jesus could not lie.

The following Sunday my parents talked me into accompanying them to church. There was to be a visiting priest that morning, and I think they felt I had a great need to receive some spiritual guidance.

This priest, unbeknownst to us, had just arrived in Colorado, having left a parish on the East Coast because he felt God was calling him to return home. It just happened that his home was near my parents' in Colorado, but he had not been home for many years. He and the people in his parish in the East had prayed, and he felt God had given him confirmation that he was to go, so he had given up everything to return to Colorado to see what God wanted him to do.

On that particular Sunday morning I was feeling quite alienated and very depressed, and I went to church feeling as if it were an exercise in futility. I had quite literally grown up in this church, and had never heard anything which put any light on my present situation. These were good people, but they had never shown any evidence of having any particular intimacy with God. In other words, it seemed impossible that anyone there could even understand my life-and-death struggle, let alone have an answer to it.

The service began as usual, with everyone parroting from the prayer book. I was only partially paying attention, being consumed as I was with my desperation to understand God's will for me. Should I go back to California, or should I contact the Colorado Unification Church? Those seemed to be the only possible options at the time.

The service proceeded, and the new priest approached the pulpit to deliver his sermon. He just stood there for a moment, looking each person in the eye. Finally his eyes rested on me, and he looked deeply into my eyes as he said quietly but very forcefully, "Do you have any idea how very much Jesus Christ loves you?" I caught my breath, and for a reason so deep that I could not even fathom it, I began to weep. I cannot even remember what else he said, or how the service ended, for I wept through the entire time. I was embarrassed, but I could not get control of myself. Finally I realized I was experiencing a very foreign emotion, and I could not label it for quite a while, but I finally recognized it as being *hope*. I realized it had literally been years since I had experienced hope; yet, I could not understand why I felt it at that time.

After the service, I leaned over to my mother, and whispered, "I don't understand it, but I can feel the presence of God in that man." This statement troubled me greatly, for I could not think of a time other than once when I had been in this same church before leaving for California, when the Bishop of Colorado had been present for a confirmation service, that I had experienced the presence of God in another person. I certainly had never felt it in anyone in the Unification Church. So, my thought troubled and angered me, and I pushed it aside. As I was getting ready to leave with my family, the priest came up to me.

"I feel very strongly that you are in deep trouble. Is there anything I can do to help?" he asked. I felt indignant, but because of the presence of God which still lingered in the room, I forced myself to try to be polite.

"No, not trouble," I answered. "I am a member of the

Unification Church, and I will be returning soon." He looked at me again, and I felt myself flinch, though I could not imagine why. Maybe Satan was using this man right now to try to deceive me, and yet I could not forget how strongly I had felt God in him earlier.

"Tell me one thing," he continued, "do you believe the Bible is the Word of God?"

"Yes, I do," I answered. The "Divine Principle" was an extension of the Bible in the same way that the New Testament was an extension of the Old Testament, I had been taught. I believed that it was also a greater revelation of God than the Bible, but it was totally consistent with the Bible.

He peered at me and asked, "Well then, would you be willing to read the Bible with me?"

For some inexplicable reason, a sudden anger came over me. "Well, I'm leaving before long, but I'll read it with you until then." It occurred to me that maybe God wanted this man to hear the "Principle" for some reason, so we set a time for him to come to my parents' house the following day.

The days which followed were terribly frustrating for him, I'm certain, because I felt a tremendous hostility toward him, but I assumed God had some reason for bringing him into my life. Every Scripture he read, I had an argument for, according to the "Divine Principle." He forged onward, and I continued to see everything he read in the light of what I had been taught. It occurred to me about that time that maybe God was answering my prayer. This man had the Bible and Jesus Christ, and I had the "Divine Principle" and Sun Myung Moon, so I determined to find out once and for all who was the King. I therefore steeled myself for battle.

It was at this time that the assaults of fear and terror

and the seeing of dark forms increased again, and I came to the point where I lived in constant fear and horror. Somehow I revealed this problem when I was talking to the priest, and he said immediately that if I ever felt the need for him to pray that I was to call him no matter what time it was.

Shortly after this discussion with him, I had a day which was nearly unbearable. When the priest came that afternoon, he sensed it in me and asked if I would let him pray and, out of sheer desperation, I consented. He laid hands on me and began to pray with tremendous authority. "In the name and authority of Jesus Christ, I command that these forces of fear and torment be gone." He then began praying in a language which was foreign to me. Immediately, I had the certain knowledge that he was praying in Hebrew. It confused me, but I felt that it was wonderful that he had learned to pray in Hebrew.

As he prayed, I felt the oppression lift suddenly and totally. I was in complete awe. For over three years I had been sprinkling "holy salt" and praying in the names of the "true parents" and singing "family songs" to do battle with these forces of darkness, and never had I seen any of these things really work with authority. Usually, my problem abated somewhat, but it never really left. For example, I remembered an incident during one of the training sessions when a young man attended who turned out to be possessed by demons. He began to rant and rave and practically foam at the mouth and claimed to be the Messiah returned. Of course the brothers had grabbed him, but it took four or five of them to just hold onto him. They had wrestled him outside and began praying, but the young man only got worse. Finally, they had to lock him outside the gate.

But here was this one priest with me, taking the authority in the name of Jesus Christ, and the demons obeyed him immediately. I was stunned and confused. I knew that this was supposed to be a new dispensation which no longer was exemplified by miracles as was Jesus' dispensation, but if we were the followers of the true Messiah, we should have authority over satanic elements in his name. Yet the "holy salt" was almost ineffective against their assaults, as were the songs and prayers. How could this be?

The assault of fear and confusion returned after a short while as I newly grasped the "Divine Principle" and tried to use it to explain away the inconsistencies I had experienced. On another afternoon, soon thereafter, despair became overwhelming. I could not get beyond my teachings, and yet the pain of what I felt I was called to do was consuming me. I called the priest's house, and a young man who lived with him answered and informed me that the priest was not at home but that he, Paul, would come over at once. He arrived within minutes and asked what was happening to me. I explained my overwhelming fear and sense of despair and confusion. He laid hands on me and prayed in the name and authority of Jesus Christ, and began to speak in another foreign language.

I could feel the power of God sweep through me, and an incredible sense of peace settled over me as he prayed. Again, I was amazed at the power of his prayer. It gave me chills, and I wept quietly as he finished praying. Afterward, Paul sat and talked about this man Jesus, and what He had done in his own life and concluded by telling me that the Lord had told him to give me a Scripture, and that I was to cling to it and claim it whenever I felt fear. He explained that fear never comes from God, and cited various passages of Scripture to point out instances stating that God does not give a spirit of fear.

He then told me to get my Bible, which was the one my parents had given me before I joined the Unification Church. We turned to the tenth chapter of Luke, beginning in the seventeenth verse, "The seventy-two came back rejoicing. 'Lord,' they said, 'even the devils submit to us when we use your name.' He said to them, 'I watched Satan fall like lightning from heaven. Yes, I have given you power to tread underfoot serpents and scorpions and the whole strength of the enemy; nothing shall ever hurt you. Yet do not rejoice that the Spirits submit to you; rejoice rather that your names are written in heaven'" (Jerusalem). Then Paul left.

I went into the living room and sat down with my Bible. I read the verse over and over. How could this be? Right there in the Bible, in the Gospel of Luke, which was one of the books which we considered to be reliably written, Jesus himself said that He had seen Satan fall like lightning from heaven. The "Divine Principle" taught that, first of all, Satan fell on earth, not in heaven, but that was not the worst of it. According to the "Divine Principle," Jesus did not even exist at the time of Satan's fall. How could Jesus have seen Satan fall, and how could Jesus have been in heaven to see the fall? My mind swirled in confusion and panic. I cried out to God to clarify it all to me.

All of these things had happened within a few days. As the time of my departure approached, I felt more and more panic and fear, but I could not understand why. Maybe it was Satan trying to keep me away from God and the Unification Church. A call came from the airline, and my heart was gripped with fear. They said that they had overbooked the flight and that I could not possibly get on it; I would have to wait another two weeks before I could get a flight back to the Bay Area. My worst fears had come true! I was literally trapped in Montrose. The cast was still on my leg, and it had to come off immediately so that I could begin therapy, or else I would not have the proper use of my knee. I knew that when the cast came off, I would be even more helpless and weak until I learned to bend my leg and walk again.

I called the Hearst Street house in Berkeley and spoke to Edie, explaining my situation. She seemed greatly disturbed, and she promised to call frequently to help me keep my courage and strength.

The priest continued to visit, and there were times when I wanted to hit him. The battle was really on as far as I could tell! For example, each day he would pinpoint something else in the Scriptures which was totally opposed to what the "Divine Principle" taught. I was not about to let him know that though, so I just fought the inconsistencies within myself. I felt a rage at everyone around me, and perceived them as being tools of Satan to weaken me and rob me of my salvation. In addition, I argued constantly with everyone, for my family had begun pointing out the things about the Unification Church and about Moon which were inconsistent with the teaching or which they felt were just plain evil. The rage was inside me all the time, and it was all I could manage to be civil to anyone. I felt trapped and hopeless in a way I had never felt before, and I was so totally alone.

I did not trust the priest at all despite the power of the Lord which I had seen in him, and the Scriptures he had shared with me, and I felt my parents were tools being used by Satan to deceive me. Because of this, even when they would come upon something which did indeed seem to discredit or disprove the validity of the "Divine Principle" or the Unification Church, I did not dare to make any decisions based on what they said. I realized that my only hope was to find out what the Bible really did say, so I set out on a frenzied search of the Scriptures.

There was a man who was a friend of the family who took a great interest in my struggle. He had at one time pursued the Catholic priesthood, and we spent hours discussing the nature of God. Still, I just could not sort out who God really was. I did not trust Him at all, because if He was the God of the Unification Church, He was a cruel, heartless, vengeful and weak God who depended on mankind to achieve His will on earth. That put the burden on my shoulders and did not in any way make Him an Almighty God. I began to question the suffering of the world, and to see it in a new light. If God allowed that suffering for the reason of indemnity, He was indeed at the mercy of Satan's influence on man, and that made Satan more powerful on earth than God was. If this were true, I was going to have to grit my teeth and "fight it out" in spite of Satan and God, for they obviously had no capacity for mercy. That made God a weakling who was not to be trusted.

Yet the God I read about in the Scriptures was opposite in nature to the one I had come to know in the Unification Church. Who was I to believe? Day after interminable day I struggled with that question, and I found myself getting into Scriptures considered not credible by the Unification teachings. The Apostle Paul was not considered reliable in his interpretations because of his Jewish outlook. That was a totally irrational idea, because all of the apostles were Jewish, and it was Paul's unique position to reach out to the Gentiles with the Word in a manner which could be understood by them. But we were not to question any of the irrational ideas they presented.

One day I was reading the letters of the Apostle Peter when I happened to find a statement by him about the teachings of Paul. Peter not only agreed with them, but he spoke pointedly of the true wisdom given to Paul in his writings, and said that many deceivers distorted Paul's writings to their own destruction. I also read that Luke, who was considered reliable by the "Divine Principle," was a companion and helper to Paul. Now if Luke was credible, he must have thought Paul to be credible also, or he would never have been a companion in Paul's travels and teachings. I considered these facts for a while and then began to read the teachings of Paul. There I found instance after instance of teaching which disproved the Moon doctrines. Not only that, I began to find that the Scriptures quoted by the "Divine Principle" from Paul's letters had been taken completely out of context and could not possibly mean what the "Principle" said they meant when they were taken in context.

Grave doubts began to arise in my mind about the validity of the "Divine Principle." I reread the Gospel of Luke, and found a tremendous inconsistency right in this Gospel which the "Divine Principle" quoted so extensively. In the twenty-fourth chapter, beginning in the thirty-sixth verse, Luke destroyed one of the basic teachings of the "Divine Principle." Specifically, we had been taught that Jesus' resurrection was solely a spiritual resurrection, and that He had been resurrected only in a spiritual body, yet this Scripture said, "And while they were telling these things, He Himself stood in their midst. But they were startled and frightened and thought that they were seeing a spirit. And He said to them, 'Why are you troubled, and why do doubts arise in your hearts? See My hands and My feet, that it is I Myself; touch Me and see, for a spirit does not have flesh and bones as you see that I have' " (NAS). I was stunned, and read it over several times. What could it mean? According to Scripture, that doctrine of the "Divine Principle" was a lie. If that part was a lie. . . .

The anger and confusion and frustration increased. I found that my whole sense of reality was threatened and crumbling around the edges. I believe that Edie was sensing this when she called, and that the "family" in Berkeley was becoming concerned. I began hiding out when she called, and always hung up with the determination that Satan was playing tricks on me, and that I had better get back as soon as possible to the group.

One evening the phone rang, and as I answered, I realized that it was Micah on the other end of the line. My heart ached, and I longed to be back in Boonville with none of this confusion and turmoil happening. I wished I could just go back and have things as they had been. His voice had an almost mesmerizing effect on me, and I felt all my questions and doubts melt away. He asked me when I was coming back. I said I didn't know, that there were complications with my flight schedule. I told him that the children were staying with my parents, and he seemed very pleased. Yet I had to tell him, in the end, what was happening. I said that I had been reading the Scriptures and that I had some grave doubts about the "Divine Principle." He answered that my doubts were about myself, not the "Principle." He went on to remind me that while I was absent, I was not "actualizing" or working directly for God, and so my spirit was not receiving elements of life, and was literally dying. He then said that I had better get back to Berkeley as soon as possible. I weakly agreed, and when he hung up I was completely devastated. If I had been at all physically able, I would have walked out the door that minute and found some way to return to Berkeley. But I was helpless. I could not use my leg at all, and that meant I could not move anywhere with any speed at all. I cried bitterly, and went to look at myself in the mirror, to determine if I could see the effects of my spirit's dying. I became impossible to live with, and spoke only of going back. The anger at my parents, and my feelings of being trapped and helpless, were tremendously magnified. Because of this, my parents forbade me to answer the telephone. I was both angry and relieved, and felt suddenly exhausted. I had still tried to retain some facsimile of the schedule in my parents' home. It was not comfortable for me simply to sit and talk or to do anything else, unless it was to study the Scriptures. I tried to keep myself busy all the time, and I would stay up reading and praying until very late at night so I would not get too much sleep.

My physical therapy sessions became a prime way to pay some heavy indemnity in that the process of getting my knee to bend again was slow and excruciating. I would pray and offer the pain up as indemnity every day until I blanched and broke out in a cold sweat and nearly passed out many times. The condition of the indemnity that I offered up was again to be released from Satan's deception, whatever it was.

I decided that until I could come to a decision about these discrepancies in the Bible and the "Divine Principle," I would not go back. And as time passed, I came to realize that there were dozens of cases of Scriptures being used to prove the "Divine Principle" which were taken completely out of context. It enraged me, to say the least, because I had been lied to, and now my safe, secure perception of reality was being shattered. I wanted to lash out and punish someone—but who? And then my anger began to turn on God himself. How could He let me be deceived that way when I had been earnestly seeking Him in the first place? Just what kind of God did we have anyway?

It appeared the only way to find Him was to discover who Jesus really is. My Bible study was renewed with a different focus. I prayed that the Father would show me who this Jesus really is, what He really did, and what He accomplished.

About that time, I had a visitor who was to change my life, an old friend, Danny, who had grown up across the street from me. He had come back to the Western Slope from Colorado Springs to a family funeral, and on a whim he had called to see what had happened to me. I answered the telephone and invited him over, primarily out of curiosity. We talked for hours, and decided that neither of us would ever get married again, for his marriage had ended in betrayal, and he felt just as bitter as I did about the whole thing. I also realized that he really seemed to have no interest in God, and that was the only thing I was interested in at the time. As he left, he promised to come back and see me. Frankly, I didn't believe him, and I wasn't sure I cared.

Time dragged on and Joshua, in his tremendously weakened condition, contracted pneumonia and was hospitalized twice. The emotional drain of this and the struggle I had been engaged in was overwhelming, and I withdrew into a state of feeling drugged and terribly tired. I simply could not handle the weight of the world on my shoulders any more, and I drifted into reading *National Geographic* magazines to escape. It was the first time in three and a half years I had read anything which was not directly concerned with God and salvation. I felt tremendous guilt, but also felt as if I had blown a fuse. I needed some time to pull myself back together after the trauma of having Josh so sick. Again I felt great anger with the priest I was working with. He was pushing the salvation message at me the same way the cult had pushed their doctrine, I thought. Yet I had a need to hear this truth. After a while I began pursuing the Word with renewed zeal; I realized that despite the lies, the cult had been right about one thing; life was worthless without God. Nothing had any real meaning without God, and I only wanted to live if I could serve Him.

Soon after that realization, I knelt (as well as I could on my still partially stiff leg) and prayed fervently. "Jesus, I just can't do it. Not only have I almost destroyed myself, but I have nearly destroyed two of your children. I've been part of a tremendous lie about you, and have helped to bring others into that lie. There is no hope for my life except you. Please forgive my sins. There are so many of them, but you have promised to forgive us if we ask. Please come into my heart and my life and take over. Please make right the mess I have created. Jesus, just take my whole life."

It had been nearly three months from the time I had

come home until the time I prayed this. As I look back, so much of that time seems dark and confused. There were many times when I knew that the Unification Church was based on a lie and had used me in the worst way, and then I would pick up the "Principle" book, or hear a song we had sung, or receive a letter from one of the members, and all that conviction would evaporate, and suddenly I would not know what was real or what the truth was. I was on a constant swing from knowing the truth as it was explained in Scriptures, and being sure I had been deceived by Satan about the wickedness of the Unification Church. It was a moment-to-moment struggle to see reality. The fear was by no means gone; it would often come upon me in the dark of night and make me feel as if my sanity was being challenged. But day by day, with the constant presence of the Scriptures, my foundation in what the Bible really said became stronger, and less and less could the assaults of fear and darkness shake my certainty of what was really there.

The effects of my programming in the cult were also very manifest during this time. Making any kind of decision was nearly impossible. Everything from what to wear in the morning to what I wanted for meals was a major milestone in my day. I hated being in the position of making even the most elementary decisions and always tried to opt out by putting the decision on someone else. "What would you like for breakfast?" would be answered by, "Oh, whatever you're going to have. I really don't care." My parents caught on to this predicament quite early and set about making me take the responsibility for even the smallest decisions. This was excruciating for me and left me with the feeling that I must be totally inept and weak.

I realize now that they did just the right thing to keep me from being crippled by indecisiveness the rest of my life. Related to this indecisiveness was a tremendous need to have an authority figure. I was practically begging to have someone tell me what to do, and when someone obliged my wishes, I responded with tremendous relief. This process was taking place on a practical, day-to-day level, but the ultimate question about whether the cult was a lie had to be settled by no less of an authority than God himself.

Even after I gave my life to Jesus, I still had major problems to confront. I found that my life seemed to be mired down by inane activity. For so very long I had felt that my life was only worthwhile if I was "actualizing"—fund raising, witnessing, or being used in a training session—that life as a mother and housekeeper was hard to justify. I relaxed and allowed myself to enjoy and nurture my children, but I felt strongly that I needed to do more. So, I found myself becoming restless, and at about that time my attention was diverted.

During this period of darkness and confusion, Danny had continued to come to the Western Slope every weekend. I found that when he was there, the heaviness seemed to lift. He was able to make me do something that I had not been free to do for several years. He knew how to make me laugh. I found that I looked forward to his visits more and more, and even came to the point where I really missed him when he was gone. Nevertheless, I was tremendously cautious. I had serious doubts about ever marrying again, partly because the misery and suffering of my first marriage were still fresh, and partly because we had been programmed to believe that if we ever left the church and married, it was the worst sin we could commit. I still had not completely convinced myself that Satan could not still do something horrible to me.

As the weeks passed, though, I found that life was more and more unbearable without Danny. I had another dilemma, however. I had promised God that I would not even consider marrying anyone who was not a Christian, and Danny was not. I insisted on going to church when he came over though, and so he accompanied me. On Good Friday, we went to services with my family. During the middle of the service, I noticed that Danny was crying. I was amazed, and asked him about it when the service was over. "I have realized that I really do believe all of this!" He had also accepted Jesus Christ as his Savior.

As the time passed, and as we were able to share our belief, the question of marriage came up. I was terrified, and came under terrible assaults of fear because of my past beliefs. In addition, I was beginning to feel the presence of evil around me again, and I did not seem able to take authority over it. This distressed me very much, for as I read the Scriptures, I could see that the early Christians had tremendous authority in the name of Jesus, and they also seemed to have a depth of relationship with Him that I could not reach. How could this be so? I had given my life to Him, and asked Him to be my Lord and Savior. I was living as best I could, according to what He said, and yet there was something missing.

One day in the grocery store, I caught sight of a book about some kind of phenomenon in the church today. I bought the book and found that it was about what the author referred to as the *Modern Day Pentecost*. I could not put the book down, and read it in one day. My thoughts were whirling, and I realized that the power the disciples had in the Lord was the same power that this man was describing in his book. The amazing thing was that it was not lost, and that God was relating to His people and allowing them to minister in the same ways He had promised the apostles. I returned to the Scriptures and could find no evidence at all that these gifts should have ceased. My hopes soared, for now it seemed that the encounters with God that I had had in the past could be an everyday occurrence. This deep, intimate relationship could be a reality through the power of the Holy Spirit, but I did not know where to go from there. I suddenly understood that the priest who had worked so faithfully with me, and the young man who had ministered to me in the beginning, both had had this power of the Holy Spirit released in them, so I began to ask questions.

By this time, I had been home for five months, and Danny was very serious about my making a decision about marrying him. He asked me to bring the children and come to Colorado Springs to see if I would ever want to live there. He had some friends who said we could stay in their home, so the plans were made. The question of marrying at all was still weighing heavily on me, and I was desperate to know what God's will was.

In speaking with the priest in Montrose, I had decided that if I was to marry, it would have to be someone who had been baptized in the power of the Holy Spirit, because my spiritual needs were so very great, and I was still having many manifestations of Satan's presence in my life. These were not as overt as they had once been, and they no longer had the power over me that they had had before, but they were still quite present. I felt that God was telling me that anyone not fully grounded in Christ, and with the ability to understand my problems through the Holy Spirit, and to take the authority over these powers which plagued me, would not be able to understand my situation. All of these things were in my mind as we arrived with Danny in Colorado Springs.

We had a lovely stay, and I liked the city very much. Shortly after we arrived, we were in a store and another book caught my eye. It was called *The Holy Spirit and You*, by Dennis Bennett. I felt that God was pulling at me to buy it, so I did.

It was a Saturday, and we looked for a body of believers to worship with the next day. Danny had spent all his weekends in Montrose, so he did not know of a church in Colorado Springs. My parents had a friend who was a priest and was supposed to be in the city somewhere, but we could not find him. We were just driving down the street that afternoon when I spotted a church. My heart began to race, and I felt God's presence strongly. "That's the one!" I exclaimed. Danny agreed. It happened to be just a few blocks from where the children and I were staying, so we all trooped into the church the next morning for the eleven o'clock service.

As we entered the building, I felt the presence of the Lord in an overwhelming way, yet the service showed no particular life. I felt confused. As we left, the priest stopped us at the door to find out who we were and what our circumstances were. Danny told him that we were to be married soon, and that we would be living in Colorado Springs. The priest asked us if we would come in and see him the following Wednesday. He went on to say that we had come to the service at which the Holy Spirit really did not have much freedom to operate, but that at the earlier service, He had much more freedom.

We did make an appointment to see this priest, and a tremendous sense of excitement began to build in me. I spent Monday and Tuesday reading the new book I had purchased while Danny was working, and I began to see more and more clearly what the Scriptures were all about in this matter, and how they applied to my life.

On Monday night, the Lord led me into the eleventh chapter of the Gospel of John, which describes the death and resurrection of Lazarus. As I read, I came to the description of Jesus' walk to the tomb, where it says that Jesus wept. The words leapt off the page at me, and I read them again. Suddenly in my mind I could see very clearly Jesus walking through all the dark, tormenting years of my recent life, and weeping over me. I was touched to the depths of my spirit, and I began to cry, for I knew without a single doubt that He had done just that.

The next day, as the children napped, I sat down with *The Holy Spirit and You* again. As I read, I rededicated my life to the Lord, and repented of and renounced all of the evil practices and beliefs I had ever been involved in, naming them one by one. As I prayed, the overpowering presence of God surrounded me. Finally, I prayed that He would baptize me in the Holy Spirit and release His power in me. As I continued to pray, a melody came into my mind and I began to hum it aloud. Then I heard sounds in my mind, just a few syllables, and I softly began to sing them to the melody. I felt completely enveloped in light and love, as if I would float right out of the room. My spirit was soaring in the greatest outpouring of the presence of God I had ever experienced. I opened my eyes, and the room was filled with golden light, and as I stared, I saw Jesus standing before me, dressed as the King.

My prayer had been answered in a way I could never have comprehended when I prayed it that dark, terror-filled night several months before. Jesus is the King, the one and only King. There never has been and never will be anyone who can take His place. He alone is worthy!

# *Epilogue*

The following day Danny and I went to see the priest of the church where the Lord had led us on the previous Sunday, and before that afternoon was over, several momentous events had occurred. First, the Lord confirmed that this was to be our church home, and we therefore made the decision to be married in this church during a Sunday worship service. In addition, Danny and the priest set the date for the marriage, and after a conversation about the baptism in the Holy Spirit in which I shared my experience of the day before, Danny received this same release of the power of the Holy Spirit while driving back to work.

We were married nearly a month later in the presence of our new church fellowship. I knew without a shadow of a doubt that God had chosen this marriage and was blessing us abundantly. The Lord had definitely directed me to our new church family, because in the months and years which followed, the children and I underwent extensive counseling in inner (spiritual) healing and deliverance. The Lord has continued to bless us abundantly in healing and growth, and in love and joy. There have been times of immense suffering over the past and its effects on our lives, but there is always victory in the Lord on the other side. And each time, I find that I have emerged more free to love and serve the Lord and others. Our God truly is a "God of power and might," as the Episcopal prayer book states. He is also tenderhearted, and loves us more than we can possibly comprehend. With every day that passes, I continue to marvel that He could love me after the lies and heresy that I perpetrated about Him. I can scarcely understand that kind of love, for there is nothing an individual can do which is beyond His love and forgiveness. He is always there to take us in His arms, if we will only turn and ask Him!

The entire purpose of my testimony, and hence this book, is to tell everyone that Jesus is indeed the King, and that He has the complete victory over the Unification Church and all the other "mind-control cults" that rob our young people of their free wills, their ability to reason and evaluate, and their very ability to live free, abundant lives as the Lord would have them live. Their souls and spirits are in bondage to these cults, and their lives are in the hands of totally ruthless systems. Great and insidious subtleties are involved, because I would have died for the belief that I was not under any form of mind control until that control was broken in me. It was only then that I was able to recognize what had been done to me, and so I can only thank the Lord for His mercy in my life and the lives of my children. But there are literally thousands of young people who continue to be under the heavy mantle of deception and heartlessness. Their spirits are crying out for release, but their minds are so fogged by programming that they are no longer in touch with their spirits. They believe that they are living a life of love and service to mankind, when in actuality they are becoming emotionless shells, parroting the thoughts, feelings and actions of the cult leader. However, Jesus Christ became the sacrificial lamb for them, too, as is foreshadowed in Leviticus and explained in the book of Hebrews. He died for their sin, deception, and tears just as He did for everyone. But they need prayer, our prayers. I recently discovered that my mother prayed for three years that God would show me the truth, and that one of my great-aunts had her entire church in Enid, Oklahoma, praying for me. I have no doubts at all about the power of prayer in these situations, because I know the Lord honors our prayers! So, please pray for these lost ones.

We, as the Body of Christ, no matter what our denominations, should be the ones who are standing against the viciousness and the outright heresy of the Unification Church and other cults. They are teaching lies about Jesus Christ, and if we as Christians don't care, who will? Jesus has already defeated Satan and this world, as stated in the sixteenth chapter of John's Gospel, but it is up to us to claim that victory.

I am calling Christians to take a stand on this issue, and if you have not already accepted Jesus Christ into your life, I am asking you to lay down your burdens, and accept the total and complete salvation He has already bought for you. He loves you just as He loves me, and He has forgiveness waiting for you just as he had for me. Please, reach out to Jesus; He is offering you life forever.

# PSALM 116

I LOVE the LORD, because he hath heard my voice and my supplications.

2 Because he hath inclined his ear unto me, therefore will I call upon him as long as I live.

3 The sorrows of death compassed me, and the pains of hell gat hold upon me: I found trouble and sorrow.

4 Then called I upon the name of the LORD; O LORD I beseech thee, deliver my soul.

5 Gracious is the LORD and righteous; yea, our God is merciful.

6 The LORD preserveth the simple: I was brought low, and he helped me.

7 Return unto thy rest, O my soul; for the LORD hath dealt bountifully with thee.

8 For thou hast delivered my soul from death, mine eyes from tears, and my feet from falling.

9 I will walk before the LORD in the land of the living.

10 I believed, therefore have I spoken: I was greatly afflicted:

11 I said in my haste, All men are liars.

12 What shall I render unto the LORD for all his benefits toward me?

13 I will take the cup of salvation, and call upon the name of the LORD.

14 I will pay my vows unto the LORD now in the presence of all his people.

15 Precious in the sight of the LORD is the death of his saints.

16 O LORD truly I am thy servant; I am thy servant, and the son of thine handmaid: thou hast loosed my bonds.

17 I will offer to thee the sacrifice of thanksgiving, and will call upon the name of the LORD.

18 I will pay my vows unto the LORD now in the presence of all his people,

19 In the courts of the LORD's house, in the midst of thee, O Jerusalem. Praise ye the LORD.

| DATE DUE | |
|---|---|
| MAY 1 – 1996 | |
| APR 27 1996 | |
| DEC 2 1 1997 | |
| DEC 1 8 1997 | |
| DEC 1 9 1999 | |
| DEC 1 3 1999 | |
| | |
| | |
| | |
| | |
| | |
| | |
| | |
| | |
| GAYLORD | PRINTED IN U.S.A. |